CONTEMPORARY CASE STUDIES

Health & Health Risks

Michael Witherick

Series editor: Sue Warn

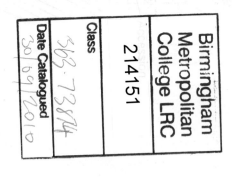
Philip Allan Updates, an imprint of Hodder Education, an Hachette UK company, Market Place, Deddington, Oxfordshire OX15 0SE

Orders

Bookpoint Ltd, 130 Milton Park, Abingdon, Oxfordshire, OX14 4SB
tel: 01235 827720
fax: 01235 400454
e-mail: uk.orders@bookpoint.co.uk

Lines are open 9.00 a.m.–5.00 p.m., Monday to Saturday, with a 24-hour message answering service. You can also order through the Philip Allan Updates website: www.philipallan.co.uk

© Philip Allan Updates 2010

ISBN 978-0-340-99181-7

First printed 2010
Impression number 5 4 3 2 1
Year 2015 2014 2013 2012 2011 2010

Front cover photograph © Adrian Brooks/Imagewise

Printed in Italy

Hachette UK's policy is to use papers that are natural, renewable and recyclable products and made from wood grown in sustainable forests. The logging and manufacturing processes are expected to conform to the environmental regulations of the country of origin.

P01714

Contents

Introduction

Part 1: Global patterns of health and health risks

Part 2: Infectious diseases

Part 3: Non-infectious diseases

Part 4: The impacts of disease

Part 5: Health and the global economy

Contemporary Case Studies

Introduction

It is said that people have three basic physical needs — food, water and shelter. These are certainly vital ingredients of the human **quality of life**. But many would say that there are other equally important aspects of our daily lives that should be included. Health would be one of these, and others might perhaps be environmental quality, freedom of speech and equal opportunities. When we use the word **health**, as just now, we are inclined to infer 'good health'. Another term that will be used as frequently in this book is '**health risks**'. Health risks are more about ill-health and the chances of contracting and suffering from disease. They are the things that threaten our good health. Just as the incidence of good health varies from one place to another, so too do health risks. **Morbidity** refers to the incidence of disease. Morbidity rates simply measure prevalence. They do not tell you whether or not people are suffering on a long-term basis from a particular disease.

Figure 1
Health and quality of life

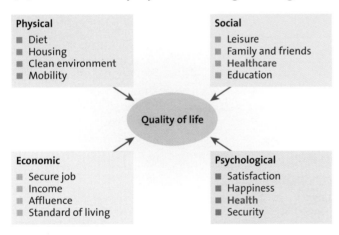

Physical
- Diet
- Housing
- Clean environment
- Mobility

Social
- Leisure
- Family and friends
- Healthcare
- Education

Quality of life

Economic
- Secure job
- Income
- Affluence
- Standard of living

Psychological
- Satisfaction
- Happiness
- Health
- Security

Table 1 *Strands of human security*

Strand	Example
Economic	Regular, properly rewarded employment
Food	Enough food to eat; a balanced diet
Health	Freedom from disease; access to healthcare
Personal	Human rights; educational opportunities
Environmental	Safe water and air; respect for biodiversity
Cultural	A sense of belonging; freedom from discrimination
Political	Democratic government; freedom from oppression

If we return to the original three basic human needs of food, water and shelter, it is significant that all have a direct bearing on health and therefore by association also on health risks (Figure 1). It is worth noting that the other facets of quality of life already mentioned also have an influence. All this tends to make health and health risks major components of our quality of life.

Finally, by way of introduction, the point should be made that the quality of life (and therefore health) is thought to increase, at an aggregate level, as a country develops. The UNDP has introduced the concept of **human security**. It is based on the idea that development, in its fullest sense, leads to a widening of people's choices. Human security is the condition that allows people to exercise these choices safely and freely. It is woven from seven strands (Table 1) and may be defined as being safe from chronic threats such as the hunger, disease and repression which unhappily remain a part of everyday life for far too many.

About this book

This book focuses on seven aspects of health and health risks:

Part 1 analyses global patterns of health, morbidity and mortality.

Part 2 puts the spotlight on different types of infectious disease.

Part 3 investigates the health risks associated with four different conditions — age, hunger, affluence and pollution.

Part 4 looks at the demographic, economic, social and environmental impacts of disease.

Part 5 examines some links between health and the global economy.

Part 6 presents a health check on the UK — what is the state of the nation's health?

Part 7 investigates a number of different modes of healthcare delivery.

Figure 2 shows the links between the parts. Each part provides the context for a selection of related case studies. At the end of each case study, the key points are summarised in italics. Some of the case studies are followed by *Using case studies* boxes. These set a range of related questions and tasks. Guidance is given as to how they might be tackled. They all aim to improve your comprehension and use of case studies so that you can enrich and support your examination answers and coursework with real-world examples.

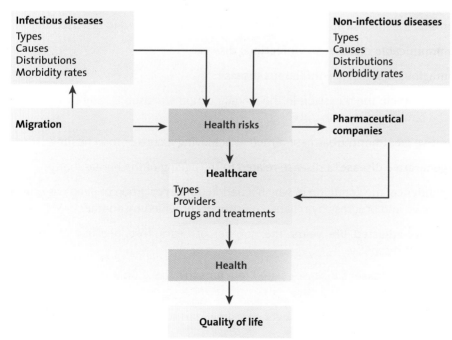

Figure 2
Links between the topics in this book

The final part of the book (**Part 8**) consolidates much of this advice and gives some additional tips on making the most of your case study material in the examination.

Underlying all parts of the book are two reference scales. One of these is the development continuum that runs from 'low-income' or 'less developed' to 'high-income' or 'more developed'. The other is the population structure continuum extending from 'youthful' to 'ageing' populations. Almost all the case studies in this book link to these two scales. The majority of them are located towards the 'more developed' and 'ageing' ends of the scales. No apology is made for this bias. It may be justified on the basis that you, the reader, live in a developed country with an ageing population. Our priority, therefore, should be to become well informed about the particular health issues and health risks that confront and challenge us in our everyday lives. That is not to say, however, that we should turn a blind eye to the issues and risks that prevail in other, less developed parts of the world with their 'younger' populations. It is a matter of achieving a sensible balance. Hopefully, the mix of case studies in this book does just that.

Key terms

accreditation: authorisation, approval or recognition that a particular drug or treatment meets agreed standards.

barefoot doctor: a person who has received a minimal medical training and who delivers basic healthcare in largely rural areas.

bilateral: in the context of aid, a one-to-one arrangement between a donor and a receiver country (see **multilateral**).

chronic: meaning deep-seated and persistent, when applied to disease.

communicable disease: see **infectious disease**.

contagious disease: see **infectious disease**.

credit crunch: the recession in the global economy caused largely by the collapse of the banking system in 2008.

curative treatment: treatment aimed at achieving a cure or total healing.

degenerative disease: a disease related to the ageing of the human body.

dependence: the condition in which a nation, region or group of people is only able to survive and progress by reliance on support provided by another.

disability-adjusted life years: the number of years 'lost' because of premature death and disability.

endogenic disease: a disease related to a person's make-up — i.e. their genes.

environmental refugees: people who are driven to migrate by environmental hazards such as persistent drought, flooding, earthquakes and volcanic eruptions.

epidemic: an outbreak of an infectious disease.

exogenic disease: a disease related to environmental conditions in the broadest sense.

generics: drugs that are produced and distributed without patent protection, and usually at much cheaper cost. They must contain the same active ingredients as the original formulation.

global economy: the evolving macro-economic system that increasingly links all the countries of the world. It is largely to do with the worldwide exploitation of resources and the production and marketing of goods and services.

globalisation: any process of change operating at a world scale and having worldwide effects. In an economic context, this is the process whereby the countries of the world are becoming increasingly involved in the expanding **global economy** through the media of trade, investment and aid.

global village: a term used to convey the idea that people around the world are being drawn closer together into a single global community.

globesity: the sudden and widespread surge in personal weight levels resulting from overnutrition and lack of exercise. Now regarded as a pandemic.

health: the condition of being sound in body and mind.

health risk: something that threatens good health, such as a **contagious disease** or insanitary living conditions.

HIC: high-income country

human security: the condition in which people have access to food, shelter, safety and opportunities.

immunisation: see **vaccination**.

infant mortality: children dying before they reach their first birthday.

infectious disease: a disease that is transmitted through direct contact with an infected individual (e.g. HIV/AIDS) or indirectly through a vector (e.g. malaria). Also referred to as a contagious or **communicable disease**.

LIC: low-income country

lifestyle disease: a disease caused by the way a person lives and related to such aspects as diet, drink and exercise.

malnutrition: an imbalance between what a person eats and what is needed to maintain good health; the outcome of a diet persistently lacking critical nutrients.

maternal mortality rate: the number of women dying during pregnancy and childbirth per 100000 live births.

MIC: middle-income country

morbidity: the incidence of sickness or disease in a population.

mortality: the incidence of death, usually expressed as the number of deaths per 1000 people.

multilateral: in the context of aid, an arrangement whereby an individual state provides help through the medium of a third party, such as the World Bank or Red Cross (see **bilateral**).

non-communicable disease: see **non-infectious disease**.

non-contagious disease: see **non-infectious disease**.

non-infectious disease: a disease that is not transmitted through direct contact with an infected individual or indirectly through a vector but results from either genetic factors or lifestyles, e.g. diabetes and cancers. Sometimes known as a disease of affluence.

obese: a person is traditionally considered to be obese if they are more than 20% over their ideal weight. That ideal weight must take into account the person's height, age, sex and build.

obesity: a medical condition in which excess body fat has accumulated to the extent that it may have an adverse effect on health, leading to reduced life expectancy.

overweight: a person with more body fat than is reckoned to be healthy; usually taken as with a body mass index of 25 or more.

palliative treatment: treatment designed to relieve the pain and distress of a disease, but not cure it. Also sometimes called symptomatic treatment.

pandemic: an infectious disease affecting large numbers of people in more than one country.

pharmaceuticals: chemicals in the form of drugs or medicines that are used in the treatment of disease.

preventive treatment: treatment in which the aim is to prevent the occurrence of a disease, as by a vaccine or a drug.

quality of life: the general condition of a person or people, reflecting such aspects as housing conditions, diet, personal security and happiness.

remittances: money sent home to family members by migrants working and living abroad.

research and development (R&D): creative work undertaken on a systematic basis in order to increase knowledge, and the use of this knowledge to devise new commercial or technological applications.

undernutrition: the condition in which people do not eat enough food.

vaccination: the administration of a vaccine by injection or ingestion to produce immunity to a disease. It is generally considered to be the most efficient and cost-effective method of preventing the spread of infectious diseases. Also referred to as inoculation or **immunisation**.

vector: a carrier, such as a mosquito, that transmits a disease or infection from one person to another.

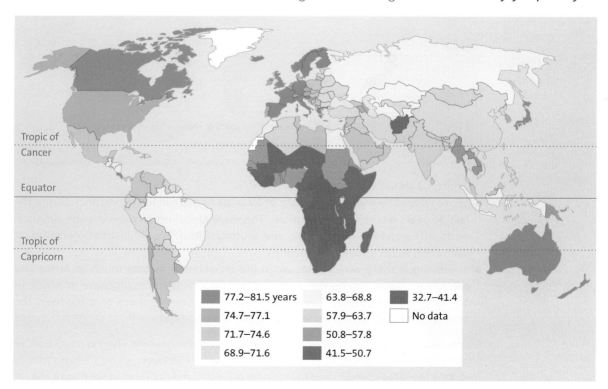

Global patterns of health and health risks

Health

There is no such thing as a global map of good **health**. The best we can do in terms of checking out the state of the world's health is to use some surrogate measures. One of the key measures of this kind is life expectancy — the healthier a population, the greater its life expectancy (Figure 1.1).

With life expectancies of more than 70 years, the 'healthiest' areas of the world appear to be Europe, North America, Japan, South Korea, Australia, New Zealand, and parts of South America, the Middle East and north Africa. In short, we are identifying what are generally acknowledged as being the more developed parts of the world — the so-called 'North'. But while large areas of the globe are shown

Figure 1.1
Global distribution of life expectancy

77.2–81.5 years	63.8–68.8	32.7–41.4
74.7–77.1	57.9–63.7	No data
71.7–74.6	50.8–57.8	
68.9–71.6	41.5–50.7	

Tropic of Cancer

Equator

Tropic of Capricorn

on the map in various shades of green, in fact those areas accommodate probably only about a third of the world's population. The majority of the world's population enjoys a lower life expectancy and level of health. The eye is caught, in particular, by the low status of much of Africa, with life expectancy at or below a mere 40 years.

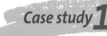

TRENDS IN LIFE EXPECTANCY

A barometer of health

By the year 2025, 26 countries will have a life expectancy at birth of more than 80 years. It will be highest in Iceland, Italy, Japan and Sweden (82 years), followed by Australia, Canada, France, Greece, the Netherlands, Singapore, Spain and Switzerland (81 years). In the UK, as in 13 other countries, life expectancy will stand at 80 years. More people will be living longer. About 800 million people — one in ten — will be over 65. Four out of every ten people dying in 2025 will be 75 or over. But there is an ironic twist to this situation. While this greater longevity is living testimony to rising levels of health, it is more than likely that 'silvering' populations will be making greater demands on those healthcare services provided specifically for the elderly. Health and providing for it will remain a major public expenditure.

Figure 1.2
Main movers in life expectancy, 1970–2009

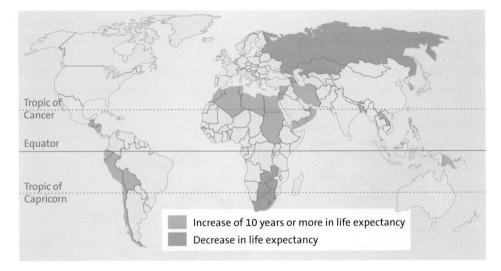

Figure 1.2 shows two categories of country:

■ Those where there was an increase of 10 years or more in life expectancy during the last 30 years of the last millennium. The main global areas were in Latin America, north Africa and the Middle East, and southeast Asia. We are justified as regarding such areas as becoming more healthy.

■ Those where there was a decrease in life expectancy, as over much of Africa and the former Soviet Union. The spread of HIV/AIDS was the main cause in Africa. In the former Soviet Union, it was the social and economic chaos that followed the transition from communism to varying degrees of capitalism.

*Overall, average life expectancy is rising slowly, but not everywhere. There is no guarantee that the trend in life expectancies will always be upwards. However, rising life expectancies may be interpreted as indicating rising levels of health and falling levels of **health risk**.*

Question

Referring to Figure 1.2, describe the distribution of those countries showing increases in life expectancy of less than 10 years.

Guidance

Having described the spatial pattern, you might refer to Figure 1.1 to see whether the countries have anything in common in terms of their present levels of life expectancy.

Another possible indicator of health, but inversely, is the **infant mortality** rate. This is the number of children who die before their first birthday per 1000 live births. In developed countries, rates have been reduced significantly by improvements in healthcare and living conditions. Rates remain persistently high, however, over much of Africa and parts of central and southern Asia (Figure 4.3, *Case study 29*). On this evidence, we may say that the remainder of the world enjoys relatively good health, with most babies surviving long enough to enjoy an adult life.

Health risks

We can also use Figure 1.1 to show the other side of the coin, namely those areas where life is most threatened by health risks. All we need to do is focus on those parts of the globe with low life expectancies. But what other measures of health risk are there? Although they are far from perfect, there are three possible measures — mortality rates, morbidity rates, and disability-adjusted life years. They give at least the 'feel' of the global situation.

Mortality rates

The argument behind using showing Figure 1.3 is that high mortality rates are likely to be associated with a high incidence of health risks.

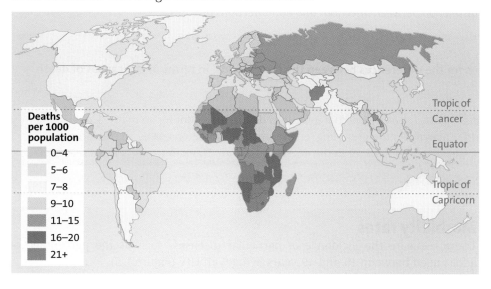

Figure 1.3
Global distribution of mortality

Deaths per 1000 population
- 0–4
- 5–6
- 7–8
- 9–10
- 11–15
- 16–20
- 21+

Tropic of Cancer

Equator

Tropic of Capricorn

Divided by numbers and cause

The two pie charts in Figure 1.4, one for developed and the other for developing countries, reveal two contrasting worlds as far as the number of deaths and their causes are concerned. The much higher figure of 40 million deaths in 1 year in developing countries is a function of two factors, namely the larger total population and a significantly higher death rate.

Figure 1.4
Main causes of death in the developed and developing worlds (2000)

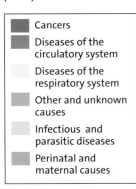

Cancers

Diseases of the circulatory system

Diseases of the respiratory system

Other and unknown causes

Infectious and parasitic diseases

Perinatal and maternal causes

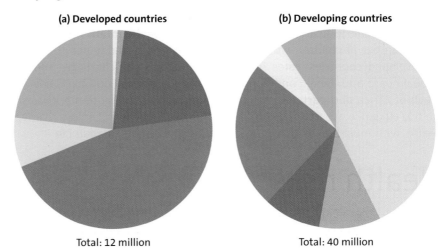

(a) Developed countries

(b) Developing countries

Total: 12 million   Total: 40 million

In terms of the main causes, the major difference between the two worlds is the dominance of **non-infectious diseases** of the circulatory system (heart) in the developed world and of parasitic and **infectious diseases** in the developing world. In the latter, HIV/AIDS is a significant killer (*Case study 34*). Another noticeable difference is that the various types of cancer are a much more prominent cause of death in developed countries.

Crucial to this comparison of the causes of death in the two 'halves' of the world is the distinction between infectious and non-infectious diseases.

2 **Using case studies**

Question

Suggest reasons for the differences between the two 'worlds' in terms of the causes of death.

Guidance

Start by looking at Figure 1.4. Why is it that infectious diseases account for so many deaths in the developing world? Think about the prevailing 'environmental' conditions. Why should lifestyle be a more conspicuous mortality factor in the developed world? Think in terms of the diseases of affluence.

Morbidity rates

These measure the incidence of particular diseases, such as the percentage of adults aged between 15 and 49 years living with HIV (Figure 1.5).

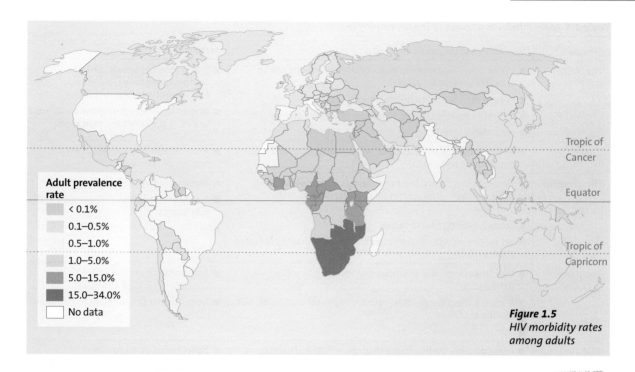

Figure 1.5
HIV morbidity rates among adults

Adult prevalence rate
- < 0.1%
- 0.1–0.5%
- 0.5–1.0%
- 1.0–5.0%
- 5.0–15.0%
- 15.0–34.0%
- No data

Tropic of Cancer

Equator

Tropic of Capricorn

INFECTIOUS DISEASES OF THE DEVELOPING WORLD

Case study 3

A frightening catalogue

Table 1.1 (see page 6) is a list of the principal infectious diseases that have high morbidity levels and account for over 40% of deaths in the developing world. The point needs to be made that around half of these diseases used to occur in what are now developed countries. Of the diseases listed, only HIV/AIDS is a significant killer in that part of the world.

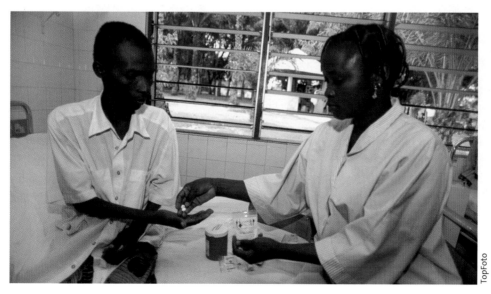

Figure 1.6
A man suffering from HIV/AIDS receives medication at a clinic in Benin, Africa

TopFoto

Table 1.1 *Main infectious diseases of the developing world*

Disease	Symptoms and prognosis	Associated factors
HIV/AIDS	■ HIV removes resistance to opportunistic infections and so prepares the way for AIDS ■ Weight loss, diarrhoea and swollen glands ■ It is estimated that nearly 35 million people are HIV-positive ■ Incurable	■ Transmitted by sexual contact, contaminated saliva, blood and hypodermic needles ■ No particular environmental conditions, but most prevalent in urban areas
Cholera	■ Severe vomiting and diarrhoea, which can quickly lead to dehydration and death	■ Associated with poor sanitation and scarcity of safe water
Dengue fever	■ Occurs in four forms. Most commonly causes painful joints, fever and rash: in fatal form there is bleeding from the mouth and nose ■ Some 2.5 billion people at risk ■ No vaccine; no specific treatment; no cross-immunity between the four forms	■ Transmitted by mosquito ■ Poorly drained areas in the tropics and sub-tropics
Diarrhoea diseases	■ Can range from mild diarrhoea and vomiting to acute dehydration ■ Probably affect the greatest number of people worldwide, but usually not fatally ■ Curable by antibiotics	■ Transmitted by touch and by contaminated food and water ■ No particular environmental conditions
Malaria	■ Fever, possibly leading to liver/kidney failure and heart/lung complications ■ 270 million people affected ■ Incurable, but preventive drugs available	■ Transmitted by mosquito ■ Poorly drained areas in the tropics and sub-tropics
Measles	■ Severe catarrh, spots inside mouth. Epidemics every 2–3 years ■ Mostly children affected; about 1 million deaths each year ■ Vaccine available, but may not provide lifelong protection	■ Spread by coughing and sneezing ■ No particular environmental conditions
Polio	■ Affects central nervous system and can lead to paralysis ■ Estimated 10 million physically handicapped survivors ■ Effective vaccine available	■ The virus is excreted in faeces, so the disease is most common in areas of poor sanitation
Sleeping sickness	■ General debilitation ■ 140 million people infected ■ Few effective drugs	■ Transmitted by tsetse fly ■ Most prevalent in humid tropical areas
Typhoid	■ High fever, rash and possible inflammation of the spleen and bones ■ 16 million cases a year ■ No long-lasting vaccine, but can be checked by antibiotics	■ Transmitted through contaminated food and water
Tuberculosis (TB)	■ Fever, weight loss and spitting blood ■ 9 million new cases each year ■ Was curable by antibiotics	■ Spread by coughing and sneezing ■ Bad housing, poor diet and unhealthy environment
Yellow fever	■ Aching muscles, headache and fever; can attack kidneys and heart ■ Reduced mortality due to immunisation	■ Transmitted by mosquito ■ Tropical rainforests of Africa and South America

Perhaps the most important aspects of this catalogue of infectious diseases are that:
■ *nearly half of them can be checked or cured by* **vaccination (immunisation)**
■ *the remainder that cannot be checked are particularly lethal*

Question

Which of the infectious diseases in Table 1.1 rely on a vector for their transmission?

Guidance

Those that rely on insects are fairly obvious, but what about those transmitted by contaminated food and water?

Disability-adjusted life years (DALYs)

DALYs refer to the number of years lost because of premature death and disability. In short, it is an indicator of health risk and burden of disease. Table 1.2 gives some hints about the aggregate situation in global regions. DALYs per million people is the better indicator, with Africa again at the top of the table, followed by southeast Asia and the Middle East. As with morbidity rates, this measure works best when related to specific health risks or social behaviour. *Case study 4* looks at maternal mortality associated with childbirth — a major contributor to DALYs in the developing world, while *Case study 5* focuses on a health risk that is rather more evenly spread across the globe in terms of its incidence and consequences — alcohol abuse.

Global region	Total DALYs (000s)	DALYs per million people
Africa	1894	3071.5
Southeast Asia	2572	1703.5
Middle East	768	1586.5
Latin America and Caribbean	92	188.5
Western Pacific	169	111.4
Developed countries	8	8.9
WORLD	**5517**	**920.3**

Table 1.2
DALYs for global regions, 2000

MATERNAL MORTALITY

Case study 4

An uneven health risk

Figures released in October 2007 by the UN and the World Bank showed that the total number of women dying during pregnancy or childbirth decreased slightly between 1990 and 2005 – from 576 000 to 536 000. This means that every minute somewhere in the world today a woman dies from causes related to pregnancy and childbirth.

This small global decline in the **maternal mortality rate** (the number of deaths related to childbearing per 100 000 live births) is mainly due to the further lowering of rates in countries that already enjoy relatively low levels of maternal mortality. Maternal mortality is declining in middle-income countries. However, those low-income countries with the highest initial levels of such deaths have made virtually no progress in reducing maternal deaths.

Of all the health indicators, the one that shows the greatest difference between the rich and poor countries is the maternal mortality rate. Ninety-nine per cent of all maternal deaths occur in developing countries, primarily in Africa and south Asia (Table 1.3). The probability that a 15-year-old female will die from a complication related to pregnancy and childbirth during her lifetime is highest in Niger (one in seven). This contrasts strongly with the lowest lifetime risk of one in 48 000 recorded in Ireland.

Table 1.3
Maternal mortality, 2005

Global region	Maternal deaths per 100 000 live births	Number of maternal deaths	Lifetime risk of maternal death (1 in …)
Developed regions	9	960	7 300
Former Soviet Union	51	1 800	1 200
Developing regions	450	533 000	75
Africa	820	276 000	26
Asia	330	241 000	120
Latin America	130	15 000	290
Oceania	430	890	62
WORLD TOTAL	**400**	**536 000**	**92**

The causes of maternal mortality are well known. Three-quarters of maternal deaths result from direct obstetric complications such as obstructed labour, septicaemia and haemorrhaging. Most of the remainder are due to 'indirect' causes, such as malaria, hepatitis, diabetes and heart disease, which can adversely affect a woman's health, particularly during childbearing. Worldwide the most common cause of maternal mortality is haemorrhaging, but the proportion due to each cause varies between global regions.

Various factors contribute to the much higher maternal mortality rates in low-income countries. They include:
■ the prevalence and debilitating effects of the 'indirect' causes noted above
■ poor diet during pregnancy
■ unhygienic childbirth conditions
■ lack of healthcare services to deal with any complications that might arise during pregnancy and childbirth

Each of these factors poses a considerable challenge. International health aid has an important role to play in reducing their impact on maternal mortality.

Maternal mortality rates provide striking evidence of the health gap that persists between the rich and poor countries of the world. Reducing that gap is proving to be no easy matter.

4 Represent the data in Table 1.3 in an appropriate cartographic or diagrammatic form.

Guidance
Is it possible to show all three indicators by means of a single map or diagram?

Using case studies

ALCOHOL ABUSE

A major health risk

Although the consumption of alcohol is an age-old tradition in many parts of the world, it is only relatively recently that we have come to realise the impacts of drunkenness and compulsive alcohol **dependence** on health. There is now a clearly established causal relationship between alcohol consumption and more than 60 types of disease and injury. Alcohol abuse is estimated to cause between 20% and 30% of all oesophageal and liver cancer, while cirrhosis of the liver and some types of epilepsy are other health risks. Persistent alcohol abuse shortens life, and in many cases premature death is preceded by years of a declining **quality of life**. Alcohol abuse also has serious social consequences, such as antisocial behaviour, murder, absenteeism from work and motor vehicle accidents.

Global consumption of alcohol has increased in recent decades, with all or most of the increase in developing countries. This increase is often the case in countries with little tradition of alcohol at the national level and few methods of prevention, control or treatment. But developed countries are not immune, given the increased incidence of 'binge drinking' among teenagers and young adults and lax laws about the sale and consumption of alcohol. Many argue it is time for a major educational offensive to inform people not just about the dangers to their own health but also about the wider social costs of antisocial behaviour and overloaded A and E departments in hospitals.

Alcohol abuse causes 1.8 million deaths worldwide each year (3.2% of the total) and 58.3 million DALYs (4% of the total). The burden is not equally distributed among countries, as shown in Figure 1.7. The worst areas are Russia and some east European

Figure 1.7
The burden of disease attributed to alcohol

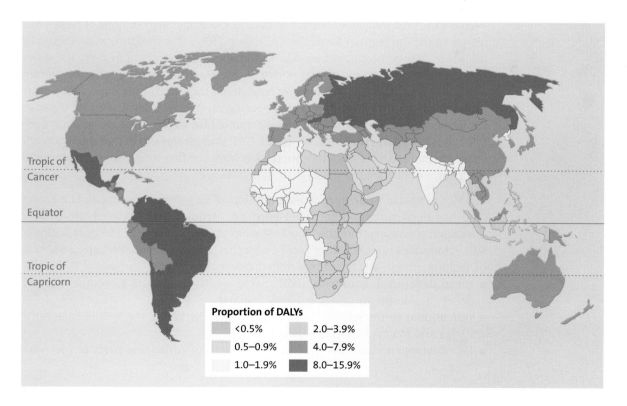

Tropic of Cancer

Equator

Tropic of Capricorn

Proportion of DALYs

<0.5%	2.0–3.9%
0.5–0.9%	4.0–7.9%
1.0–1.9%	8.0–15.9%

countries, central America and South America. But there are no grounds for complacency in the rest of Europe (*Case study 44*), North America, China and Australasia. Islam's ban on the consumption of alcohol explains the low values in the Middle East and north Africa. Elsewhere in Africa, the reason is possibly poverty.

*Alcohol abuse is a prime example of a non-infectious, **lifestyle disease** that afflicts both rich and poor people and countries. Not only is it a cause of premature death, but it also has serious social consequences.*

5 Question

Explain why alcohol abuse is both a health risk and a cost to society.

Guidance

Identify the health risks and then explore the various ways in which alcoholism adversely affects society. Can you think of ways not mentioned in the case study?

The Human Development Index (HDI)

Perhaps the best indicator we have to date of the global distributions of health and health risk is the Human Development Index (HDI). This measure was devised by the UN to assess the state of economic and social development in each and every country. It is based on the measurement of three factors — life expectancy, literacy and per capita GDP. We have already considered the value of life expectancy as an indicator of health. Literacy too has a bearing, in that with basic education comes some awareness of the causes of disease and of how to minimise the impact of the infectious ones (*Case study 12*). Per capita GDP is also relevant, in that the higher the value the more likely it is that a country will have the financial resources to provide some form of healthcare.

The HDI ranges in value from 0 (least developed) to 1 (most developed). The Brandt Line has been superimposed on Figure 1.8, dividing the so-called 'North' (the developed countries) from the 'South' (the developing countries). The distribution of HDI values does not altogether accord with this simple division. Perhaps we should be looking instead at a broad threefold division of the world:

- **most developed countries** (HDI >0.8) — North America, southern South America, Europe, Australia and New Zealand
- **transitional countries** (HDI 0.6 to 0.79) — Russia, China, the Middle East, north Africa and much of Latin America
- **less developed countries** (HDI <0.6) — much of Africa and parts of southeast Asia.

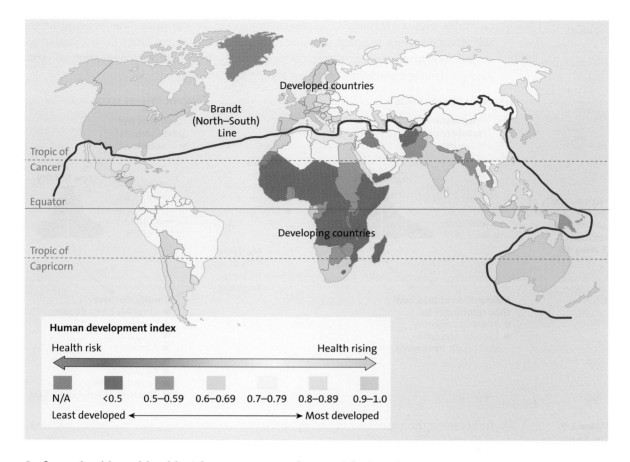

Figure 1.8
*Global distribution
of HDI, 2003*

So far as health and health risks are concerned, we might imagine two contrary gradients running alongside that of the HDI. The health gradient rises in harmony with that of the HDI, while the health risk gradient inclines in the opposite direction.

The global patterns of health and health risk that have been examined in this part of the book suggest that we live in a divided world. Strong contrasts exist between the developed and developing worlds in terms of the general level of health and the type of health risk, as well as rates of mortality and morbidity. Perhaps the most powerful single indicator of this divided world is life expectancy.

The epidemiological transition

Another factor supporting the idea of a world divided by health and health risks is what is known as the epidemiological transition. This is based on the observation that economic development has a direct impact on the health and longevity of a population through increasing levels of income, consumption and investment in healthcare. Running parallel with these impacts is a fundamental change in the nature of prevalent diseases. That change is basically from infectious diseases in less developed countries to non-infectious or **chronic** diseases in more developed countries. Figure 1.9 models the two extreme disease scenarios, one for an agrarian subsistence society plagued by infectious diseases, and the other for an industrial or postindustrial society suffering increasingly from chronic degenerative and lifestyle diseases associated with an ageing and affluent population.

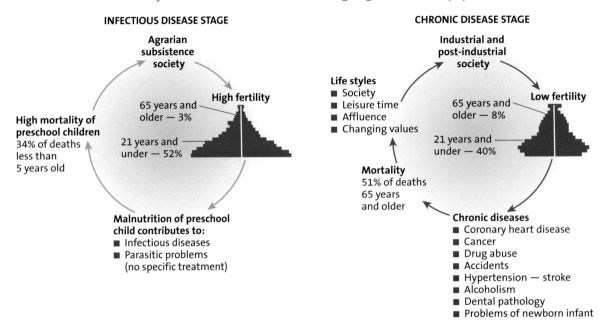

Figure 1.9
The beginning and end of the epidemiological transition

In between the extremes of the epidemiological transition, we find today's China. It is still a significantly agrarian society, but it is now well on its way to becoming an industrial society, Chronic diseases, especially those related to lifestyle, are becoming more conspicuous on maps of morbidity and mortality.

Infectious diseases

The diversity of disease

Around 1800 different diseases are currently recognised worldwide. These health risks vary, of course, in terms of their symptoms, causes, morbidity and mortality. Given the number and diversity of diseases, it is understandable that the medical profession should sort them into categories according to particular characteristics.

There are two different classifications in operation. One initially distinguishes between infectious and non-infectious diseases. But other terms are used in making this twofold distinction. They are **communicable** and **non-communicable**, **contagious** and **non-contagious**. Transmission of an infectious disease may occur through one or more pathways. The most obvious of these is by physical contact with infected individuals (as with measles or smallpox). Infecting agents may also be spread through liquids (cholera), body fluids (HIV/AIDS), contaminated objects (food in the case of typhoid), airborne inhalation (tuberculosis), or through a **vector**. The best known vector is the mosquito that carries malaria and transmits it from one person to the next by its bite (*Case study 13*).

Non-infectious diseases tend to fall into two groups: **degenerative diseases** are largely those associated with the ageing of the human body (various forms of cancer and dementia); **lifestyle diseases** are related in the developed world to such things as overconsumption of alcohol and food (**obesity**). In developing countries, equivalent diseases might be those associated with unhealthy housing (respiratory diseases) and a poor diet (**malnutrition**).

The second classification of diseases is based on an initial distinction between endogenic and exogenic diseases. **Endogenic diseases** are linked to a person's make-up — literally their genes. Examples include most forms of cancer, circulatory (heart) and respiratory (breathing) diseases, as well as degenerative diseases such as multiple sclerosis and Alzheimer's disease. They are often described as **chronic**, in that they are typically deep-seated or long-lasting. In contrast, **exogenic diseases** are linked in some way to 'environmental' conditions in the broadest sense. These conditions range from climate, housing and pollution to population densities, affluence and behaviour.

It has to be said that the distinction between endogenic and exogenic is not always clear. For example, there are diseases, largely of a non-infectious kind, whose causes are by no means certain. While cancer is generally recognised as falling in the endogenic category, it is now established, for example, that smoking (an exogenic factor) is a major cause. However, not all smokers develop lung cancer. A similarly clouded situation exists with respect to heart disease. It is regarded as an endogenic disease, but eating habits are now identified as being a major contributory factor. Because of these 'grey' areas, we will follow the first classification (infectious versus non-infectious) in the remainder of this book.

Pandemics of the past

Pandemics are outbreaks of infectious disease that spread through human populations over large areas, for example across continents and even worldwide. In contrast, epidemics are outbreaks of disease at a national scale. The UK, like all other countries, has a long medical history of **epidemics**, plagues, unpleasant diseases and pandemics.

One of those pandemics had a particularly profound impact on the UK — the Black Death of the mid-fourteenth century.

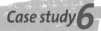 *Case study 6* — THE BLACK DEATH

A historic and epic epidemic

The Black Death came in three forms: the bubonic, pneumonic and septicaemic, each of which was a vicious killer. All forms were caused by a bacterium called *Yersinia pestis*. The main transmitters of the bacterium were oriental rat fleas carried by black rats.

The bubonic plague was the most commonly seen form of the Black Death. Up to three-quarters of those who contracted the disease were killed by it. The symptoms were enlarged and inflamed lymph nodes around the armpits, the neck and the groin. Victims experienced severe headaches, nausea, aching joints, fever of 101–105 degrees and vomiting. Symptoms took from 1 to 7 days to appear. The speed with which the disease could kill was terrifying to inhabitants of the medieval world. The fourteenth-century Italian author and poet Boccaccio claimed that the plague victims 'ate lunch with their friends and dinner with their ancestors in paradise'.

It is thought that the plague started somewhere in Asia and was brought to the Crimean port of Caffa in 1346 by Tartar traders from the steppes of central Asia. Italian merchants from Genoa, who had made Caffa into a thriving centre of trade, were probably responsible for the onward spread of the plague into Europe. It was transmitted along overland trade routes and across seas. The spread of the plague was generally northwards and westwards, passing through Italy, France, Britain, Germany, Denmark, Sweden, Poland and Finland, and eventually reaching Greenland (Figure 2.1).

It is not certain where or when the Black Death reached England. Some say that it was at Bristol, others that it was somewhere along the Dorset coast. The disease appeared in England in the summer of 1348. Once it had 'come ashore', it spread throughout Britain with amazing speed and fatal consequences. The effect was at its worst in cities, where overcrowding, poor sanitation and large rat populations helped its spread. On 1 November the plague reached London, and up to 30000 of the city's population of 70000 died from it. Over the next 2 years, the disease killed between 30% and 40% of the entire population. Given that the pre-plague population of Britain was around 5 million people, deaths from the disease may have been as many as 2 million. It has

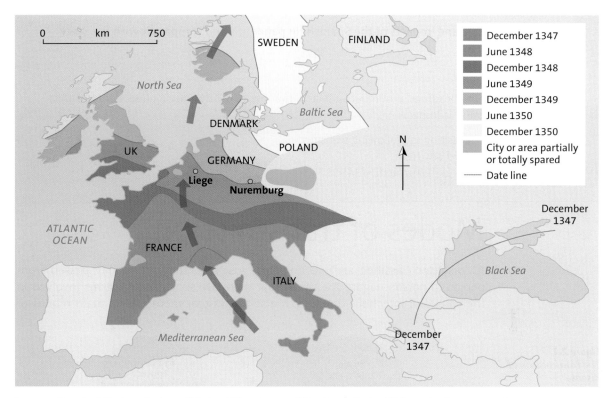

Figure 2.1
*The spread of the
Black Death across
Europe*

been estimated that up to two-thirds of the clergy of England died within a single year. They contracted the disease as they struggled to administer the last rites to victims. Peasants fled their fields and abandoned their livestock. The populations of whole hamlets and villages were wiped out and settlements abandoned.

By the end of 1350 the Black Death had subsided in Britain, but it did not die out. There were four further outbreaks in the fourteenth century, and more throughout the first half of the fifteenth century.

The repercussions of the Black Death were immense and involved much more than just the abandonment of settlements.

- The huge loss of labour not only depressed the economy but also forced people to change the way they worked and what they did for a living. Before the Black Death, for example, the main source of income in East Anglia was growing crops. However, the survivors of the plague were forced to turn to rearing sheep for wool — this required much less labour.
- The lack of labour also encouraged the invention of new equipment. Nets replaced spears as a means of catching fish — a much more efficient use of labour.
- Some believe that the Black Death was also responsible for bringing feudalism to an end. This was the system by which peasants were forced to provide labour for a lord in return for the right to farm some land. Since labour became so scarce, the survivors of the plague could be more choosey about where they worked and for whom.

The Black Death is probably the most infamous of all the pandemics ever to hit the UK. It had a profound impact on population numbers and fundamentally affected both the economy and society. Its nearest rival was probably the Spanish flu that ravaged the country and much of the world between 1918 and 1920.

Research the scale and impacts of the Spanish flu pandemic and compare it with the Black Death.

Guidance

Research under the headings of numbers affected, number of deaths, distribution, demographic impacts and economic impacts.

You might start by visiting the following websites:
http://virus.stanford.edu/uda/
http://news.bbc.co.uk/1/hi/health/3455873.stm

Modes of transmission

All diseases classified as 'infectious' are just that: they are readily passed from person to person. Figure 2.2 shows that there are six basic organisms involved in the spread of infectious diseases. It also shows that there are six main modes of

Figure 2.2
The transmission of disease

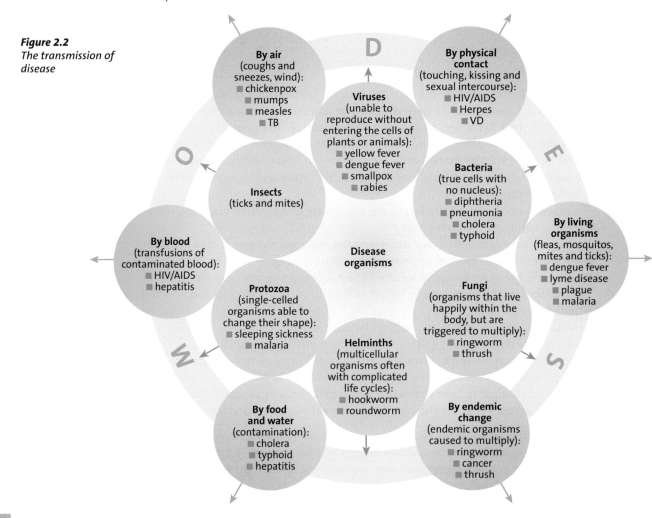

transmission. People are not just the victims of infectious diseases; they often act as vectors in transmitting and spreading such diseases. This is well illustrated by *Case study 7*.

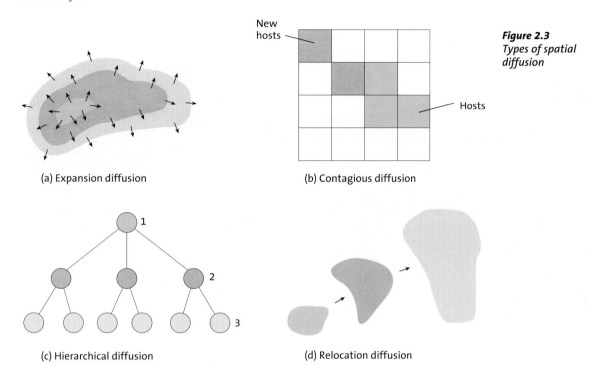

Figure 2.3
Types of spatial diffusion

(a) Expansion diffusion

(b) Contagious diffusion

New hosts

Hosts

(c) Hierarchical diffusion

(d) Relocation diffusion

The transmission of disease takes place over not only time but also space. There are four types of spatial diffusion (Figure 2.3):

■ Expansion — the infection spreads out in all directions from the point of origin.
■ Contagious — the infection is spread by direct contact, so hosts carrying the disease pass it on to new contacts.
■ Hierarchical — the infection spreads down through a particular system: for example, HIV/AIDS in the USA appeared first in the major cities and then spread to smaller cities and then towns.
■ Relocation — an infection spreads into a new area and dies out in its previous location.

THE UNHEALTHY TROPICS

Case study **7**

Part of the colonial heritage?

The tropics are frequently perceived today as inherently unhealthy places. Indeed, in colonial times, many tropical areas were referred to as the 'white man's grave'. Despite the catalogue of infectious diseases presented in Table 1.1 (page 6) and generally high mortality rates, it would be wrong to think that tropical areas are rife with killer diseases. Moreover, there is evidence that these areas were healthier before their colonisation by Europeans. Early travellers in Africa, for example, commented on the physical well-being of the native peoples.

Figure 2.4
Shanty housing in the Asian tropics — diseases once common in Europe now exist in some tropical regions due to high population densities and pollution

It was Europe that was essentially disease-ridden and it was Europeans who took the diseases abroad, for example to the Americas. Here the Amerindian population died in their millions because they had no immunity to the introduced pathogens. The diseases now found in the tropics, such as cholera, TB, leprosy and bubonic plague were — until relatively recently — widespread in urban Europe. Those diseases disappeared in Europe because of improved living conditions (clean drinking water, better sewage disposal and more hygienic housing) and better nutrition. Having been 'exported' to the tropics, the same diseases persist today, most noticeably in towns and cities where — as in Europe 200 years ago — high population densities and pollution create an environment in which infectious diseases flourish and spread with amazing speed (Figure 2.4).

This case study is a salutary reminder that while people strive to conquer infectious diseases, they are at the same time capable of spreading such diseases and changing their global distribution patterns.

7

Using case studies

Question

Explain why the diseases 'exported' to the tropics by colonial settlers were so lethal and why they have persisted.

Guidance

Think in terms of (1) immunity and (2) prevailing environmental conditions.

Some diseases can be passed from one species to another, as for example from pigs to humans and from birds to humans in the cases of swine flu (*Case studies 38 and 57*) and avian flu respectively.

Conquered diseases

One theme running through human history is the ongoing battle against health risks of the infectious kind. There have been some positive outcomes in that long history, with specific diseases being tackled so effectively that they have disappeared. Smallpox and polio are two such examples.

SMALLPOX

A success story

Smallpox is a disease caused by a virus that affects the lungs, from where the blood carries it to other parts of the body, in particular the skin, the intestines, the kidneys and the brain. It leaves deep pockmarks on the skin and can cause infertility and blindness (Figure 2.5). Believed to have originated in Africa, this highly contagious disease spread to Europe between the fifth and seventh centuries, killing millions of people.

Figure 2.5
The 'scars' of smallpox

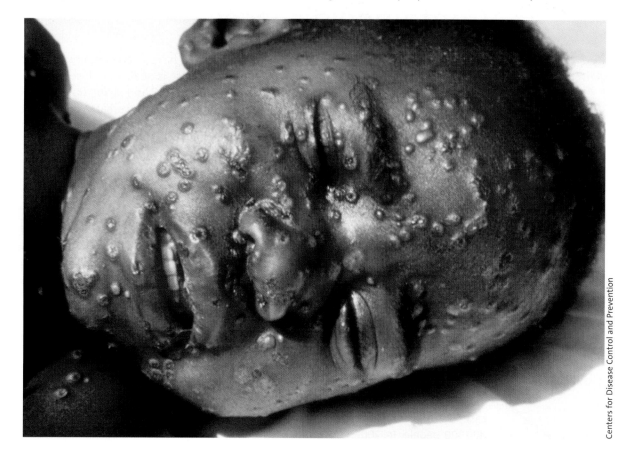

Centers for Disease Control and Prevention

The first major achievement in combating smallpox is believed to have occurred in the eleventh century, when it was discovered that people who had had the disease but survived it remained immune. This knowledge formed the basis for the practice known as 'variolation', which involved deliberately exposing healthy people to scab material from infected individuals. Some patients died as a result, but significantly more survived.

In the eighteenth century the English physician Edward Jenner noticed that milkmaids who had previously caught cowpox appeared to have an immunity to smallpox. He tested this by taking fluid from a pustule on the hand of a milkmaid with cowpox and injecting it into an 8-year-old boy. Six weeks later he exposed the boy to smallpox, who did not fall ill. This experiment led to the introduction of vaccination against smallpox, and by 1800 about 100 000 people had been vaccinated worldwide.

In 1967 the World Health Organization (WHO) launched a global campaign to eradicate the disease. A huge international vaccination programme helped to achieve this in a mere 10 years. The last reported case of smallpox was in Somalia in 1977. On 8 May 1980 the World Health Assembly declared the world free of smallpox.

Although the disease has been eradicated, the threat of its return has once again brought it to the forefront of public controversy. Should children continue to be vaccinated? Might the disease make a sudden and devastating reappearance?

Contained diseases

Other diseases have proved more resilient and at best have been contained rather than conquered (*Case study 13*). Then, just as one disease is dealt with, it seems that a new one appears out of the blue, such as HIV/AIDS, SARS and swine flu. Success in the human battle against infectious diseases has not been universal. A number of diseases that once prevailed throughout the world have largely been eradicated in developed countries, but still persist in developing countries. *Case study 9* illustrates the point that developing countries still face a range of infectious and often lethal diseases.

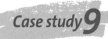

Case study 9　TYPHOID

An infection with a famous victim

Perhaps one of the most famous victims of typhoid was Prince Albert, the husband of Queen Victoria, who died of the disease in 1861. At one time, it was a major killer in Europe. It was normally associated with overcrowded housing, poor sanitation, defective sewers and inadequate washing facilities. A fractured and overflowing sewer at Windsor was the culprit in Prince Albert's case (Figure 2.6). However, the slum conditions that favoured the disease had largely disappeared in the UK by the 1930s. The infection is most commonly transmitted from human to human via contaminated food or drinking water.

Typhoid remains a life-threatening disease. It is estimated that there are 16 million cases of typhoid worldwide each year, and that its annual death toll is around 600 000 people. In 2006, 248 cases of typhoid were reported in England and Wales.

Simon Lassam/Fotilia

In half of the cases, the infection was picked up abroad by UK tourists in India, Spain, Portugal, Turkey, Egypt, Tunisia and Morocco. Of the remainder, the infection was mainly carried by immigrants and visiting family members from the Indian subcontinent.

In most cases, antibiotics are an effective treatment for typhoid. In short, there seems to be no reason why the disease should not be contained. However, one particularly worrying aspect of typhoid is the existence of chronic carriers. These are people who have contracted the disease. Although they recover, they continue to carry the disease for months, or even years. So long as they do so, they can transmit the infection to others. It is estimated that around 40% of chronic carriers respond to a long-term course of antibiotics. Unfortunately, the bacterium responsible for causing the disease has developed a resistance to commonly used antibiotics. Thus it is becoming increasingly necessary to treat carriers with either 'heavier' medicinal therapies or even surgery (removing the gall bladder, in which the disease lingers). But so long as a single chronic carrier remains untreated, typhoid will persist.

Figure 2.6
Queen Victoria's husband, Prince Albert, died from typhoid contracted from a leaking sewer at Windsor Castle

8 Question

Suggest reasons why smallpox has been completely eliminated but typhoid has not.

Guidance

Compare the sources or causes of the two diseases.

Using case studies

Emerging diseases

Undoubtedly, *the* new infectious disease of the late twentieth century was HIV/AIDS, which the world first became aware of in 1981 (*Case study 34*). There is a tendency to think that all new infectious diseases have their origins in the developing world. In the case of one new disease, however, *Case study 10* puts the record straight. What is additionally worrying is that this infection first occurred in the UK and is most frequently encountered in what we regard as our medical 'safe houses', namely our hospitals.

Case study 10 — A NEW SUPERBUG: MRSA

Methicillin-resistant *Staphylococcus aureus* (MRSA)

Figure 2.7
The global distribution of emerging diseases

The bacterium Methicillin-resistant *Staphylococcus aureus* (MRSA) was discovered in the UK in 1961 and has become known as a 'superbug' because of its resistance to many types of antibiotic used to treat infections. It seems to have taken hold in hospitals, where many patients are at risk of catching the bacteria, particularly those with open wounds, invasive devices and weakened immune systems. Hospital staff who do not

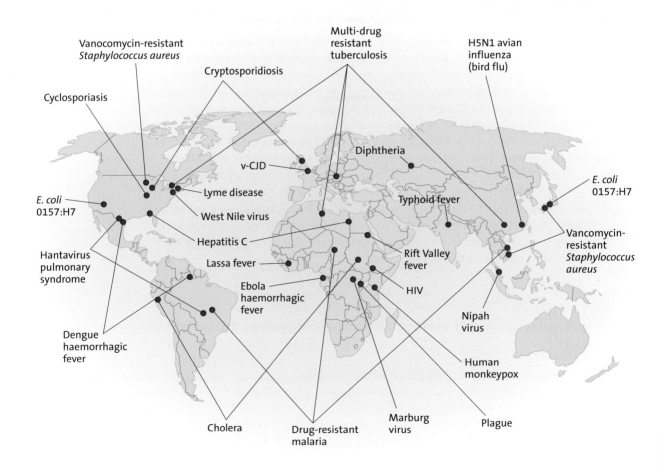

follow the correct sanitary procedures can easily transfer the bacteria from patient to patient. Visitors to patients with MRSA can also carry and spread the disease outside hospitals.

In 2005, there were 1629 MRSA-related deaths in England and Wales, and 17 000 in the USA. How MRSA evolved is not known, and the medical profession has yet to come up with an effective antibiotic.

What we see here is one example of a growing number of instances where strains of infectious disease develop resistance to particular drugs. Is this yet another case of evolution keeping ahead of modern medicine?

Figure 2.7 shows that MRSA is not the only emerging disease. Interestingly, these newcomers are not confined to the developing world.

Re-emerging diseases

Infectious diseases can be resilient and resourceful, even in the face of mass vaccination programmes. Diseases can undergo small genetic changes that help them evade vaccines, as is suspected in the cases of MRSA and swine flu. Also it only needs a few people not to participate in a vaccination programme for an infectious disease to re-emerge long after it was thought to have been eliminated. *Case study 11* provides a timely warning.

MEASLES IN THE UK
Case study **11**

A vaccine unfairly derailed

Measles is caused by a very infectious virus. Nearly everyone who catches it will have a high fever and a rash and generally feel unwell. Children usually have to spend about 5 days in bed and could be off school for 10 days. Some children are more seriously affected by measles than others. The complications of measles affect one in every 15 children, and include chest infections, fits, swelling of the brain and brain damage. In very serious cases, measles kills. In 1987, the year before an effective vaccine was introduced in the UK, 86 000 children caught measles and 16 died.

The MMR vaccine was introduced in 1988 to replace single vaccines against three very common infectious diseases of childhood — measles, mumps and rubella. A nationwide vaccination programme was launched. The programme had almost eradicated the three diseases from the UK when in 1998 a doctor suggested that there

Figure 2.8
Confirmed cases of measles in Wales, 1996–2009

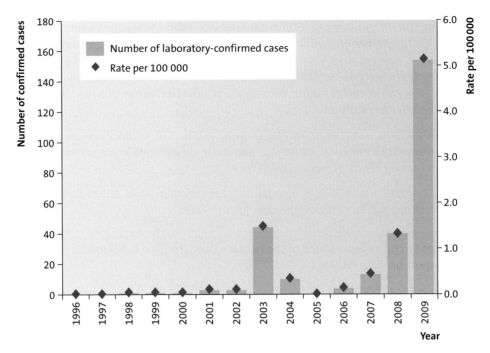

was a link between the MMR vaccine and cases of autism and bowel disease. It was not until 2008 that the General Medical Council was able to state that the vaccine was completely safe and that the risk of autism was nothing more than unfounded scaremongering.

In the years between 1998 and 2008, many anxious parents made the decision not to have their children immunised. As a consequence, the incidence of measles began to increase. Measles is such an infectious disease that a cough or a sneeze is enough to spread it, and the chances are that if they are not protected most children will catch it. It only needs one unprotected child to contract the disease, perhaps as a result of an overseas visit by them or a member of their family, and an epidemic can develop among their unprotected peers.

In May 2009, health chiefs in Wales were dealing with a 'massive' measles outbreak, with numbers already four times the highest figure recorded over the previous 13 years (Figure 2.8).

Because of parental complacency and mass media scaremongering, measles has re-emerged as a health risk in the UK. It will remain this way until every child in the country has received the MMR vaccine.

10 **Imagine that you have been asked to make a short presentation to young mothers, promoting the measles vaccination programme. What would be your four main arguments?**

Using case studies

Guidance

Focus on the benefits of involvement and the costs of non-involvement to both the child and society at large.

Sporadic diseases

Infectious diseases that are associated with particular environmental conditions, such as polluted water and contaminated food, are especially difficult to eradicate completely. For this reason, there are diseases that periodically flare up. Cholera is a typical example.

ZIMBABWE'S CHOLERA EPIDEMIC

Made by the country's economic crisis

Cholera is a disease generated by the pollution of water supplies, most often by the seepage of sewage. It is closely associated with the poorest urban areas of developing countries. A widespread cholera outbreak in Zimbabwe began on 27 August 2008. Four days later, the first case was reported in the capital city, Harare. Soon other towns were being drawn into the gathering epidemic, with rates of infection rising above 1000 cases per 100 000 people. The rapid initial spread of the outbreak was due largely to

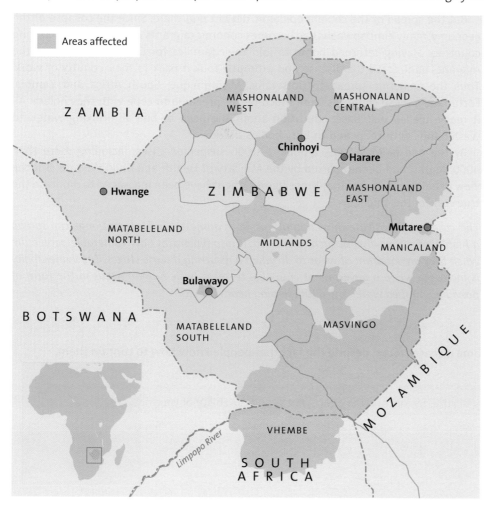

Figure 2.9
Map showing the spread of cholera in Zimbabwe and South Africa, 2008

an acute shortage of water purification chemicals, such as chlorine. The shortage was the result of the economic crisis that had brought the country to its knees — thanks to government incompetence and corruption. The country had no money with which to buy the necessary chemicals. As a consequence, inadequately treated water began to be pumped into the distribution system.

As if the breakdown of the urban water infrastructure was not bad enough, events took a major turn for the worse as urban Zimbabweans returned to their family villages en masse to celebrate Christmas. Cholera is a highly infectious disease, and soon more than three-quarters of Zimbabwe became affected. The fact that outbreaks were now occurring in rural areas presented an additional problem. Since cholera was virtually unknown in rural areas, people had little idea of what to do in order to counteract the disease, namely to consume large amounts of boiled water. Rural areas also lacked emergency treatment centres of the kind set up in urban areas by western aid organisations during previous epidemics. Additionally, the economic crisis had deprived the health service of the vehicles, fuel and staff needed to venture into the countryside to help. Villagers were so destitute that they had no means of reaching the urban cholera centres. In a population weakened by hunger, cholera can kill in 4 to 6 hours.

But the spread of the cholera epidemic did not end there. Since the collapse of the economy, many Zimbabweans had become economic migrants working in neighbouring countries. Having returned home to join their families for Christmas, many of the migrants contracted the disease and promptly took it back to their country of work. Thus the epidemic spread to Botswana, Mozambique, South Africa and Zambia. Fortunately, these countries were much better prepared to cope with the cholera. All it really needed was basic education about the need to boil all drinking water, to wash hands with soap, and to bury bodies quickly.

By the end of May 2009, around 100 000 suspected cases, including more than 4000 deaths, had been reported by the Ministry of Health and Child Welfare. But the view of aid agencies was that these figures might have been massaged to diminish the true scale of the epidemic.

This case study illustrates how migrations, both domestic and international, can spread a highly infectious disease such as cholera. It also illustrates how vulnerable people are when they are ignorant of what to do when a recurring disease strikes. The vulnerability is increased when a government is unable to meet basic human needs in the form of providing purified water and a functioning health service.

11

Using case studies

Question

Explain why some diseases recur, despite the fact that people know how to contain them.

Guidance

Think in terms of causal factors and the effectiveness and durability of vaccines.

Unconquered diseases

The media often carry reports extolling the achievements of modern medical science. Some of the above case studies provide supporting examples. However, it is sobering that the most lethal infectious disease in the developing world — malaria — remains largely untamed (Table 1.1). Prophylactics (vaccines or drugs) can only do so much by way of protection. But for malaria, as indeed that other mosquito-spread disease, dengue fever, there is no cure in sight.

| MALARIA | *Case study* **13** |

Once bitten...

Malaria is an infectious disease caused by the presence of protozoa (known as *Plasmodia*) in the red blood cells. It is a vector-borne disease transmitted by the blood-sucking female *Anopheles* mosquito. There are many species of mosquito, but it is only this one that carries the disease, and then only the females. Malaria is now confined to tropical and sub-tropical regions, particularly ill-drained areas.

When the mosquito bites, malarial parasites picked up from the last human victim carrying the disease are injected into the bloodstream and migrate to the liver and other organs of the body, where they multiply (Figure 2.10). After incubating for up

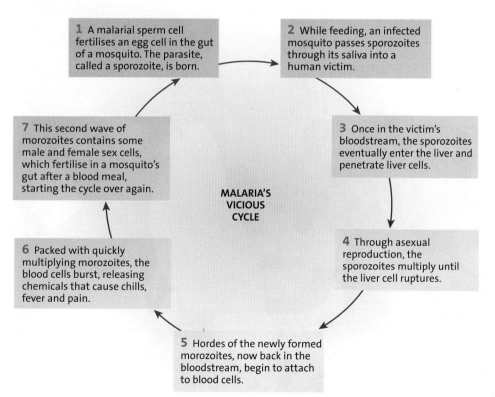

Figure 2.10
Malaria's vicious cycle

1 A malarial sperm cell fertilises an egg cell in the gut of a mosquito. The parasite, called a sporozoite, is born.

2 While feeding, an infected mosquito passes sporozoites through its saliva into a human victim.

3 Once in the victim's bloodstream, the sporozoites eventually enter the liver and penetrate liver cells.

4 Through asexual reproduction, the sporozoites multiply until the liver cell ruptures.

5 Hordes of the newly formed morozoites, now back in the bloodstream, begin to attach to blood cells.

6 Packed with quickly multiplying morozoites, the blood cells burst, releasing chemicals that cause chills, fever and pain.

7 This second wave of morozoites contains some male and female sex cells, which fertilise in a mosquito's gut after a blood meal, starting the cycle over again.

MALARIA'S VICIOUS CYCLE

to 10 months, the parasites return to the bloodstream and invade the red blood cells. Rapid multiplication of the parasites ruptures the cells, causing fever, shivering and sweating. When the next batch of parasites is released, the symptoms reappear. The intervals between bouts of fever vary with different types of malaria — four main types are recognised. Severe forms of malaria can cause liver and kidney failure, as well as brain and lung complications. The basic point with all forms of malaria is that once a person is bitten by an infected mosquito, malaria is for life.

Between 300 and 500 million new cases of malaria are reported annually, 90% of them in Africa. About 270 million people are believed to be infected at any one time. Up to 2 million people die each year from malaria and its complications, and over 2.5 billion people, almost half the world's population, are at risk of contracting the disease.

The long battle against malaria has proceeded on two fronts:

- By treatment of the habitat where the *Anopheles* mosquito breeds. This has involved either draining the offending swampy areas or spraying them intensively with DDT and similar chemicals.
- By encouraging those at risk to take preventive medication. This usually involves a daily dose of chloroquine or a weekly dose of paludrine — sometimes both. Unless it is treated in its initial stage, there is no cure for malaria. Once contracted, malaria is in the body for life.

Figure 2.11 A nurse instructs Kenyan villagers on the use of mosquito nets to prevent malaria

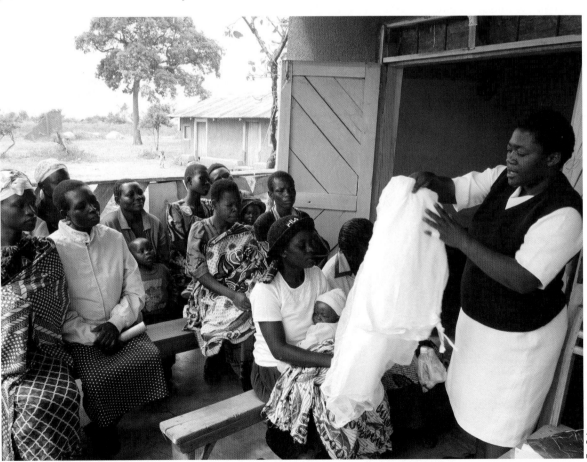

TopFoto

Contemporary Case Studies

Despite these two strategies, the sobering fact is that malaria remains one of the most prevalent and devastating parasitic diseases to afflict humans. Despite the development of new prophylactics, there have been setbacks in the battle against malaria.

- Resistance of the mosquito to DDT and other chemicals continues to spread.
- There is a growing resistance to the drugs taken by people to prevent them catching it. This applies particularly to the strain known as *Plasmodium falciparum*, which affects the brain. At present, only a few relatively new and expensive drugs (mefloquine, doxycycline and malarone) are capable of providing adequate protection, but as a result of side-effects experienced by some people they have not received universal approval.
- The cost of anti-malarial drugs is clearly an issue in developing countries and a serious obstacle to achieving the ultimate goal in the battle against malaria — namely a population in which not a single person is carrying the disease. All it takes is one carrier and one female *Anopheles* mosquito, and the vicious cycle that spreads the disease is set in motion once again.
- The fight against malaria is made more difficult by the recent discovery that global warming is encouraging malaria to creep up into the upland areas in countries such as Kenya, Ethiopia and Papua New Guinea. *Anopheles* mosquitoes are now transmitting the disease at altitudes above 2000 metres, where previously people have not needed to take precautions against it.
- The growth of international trade, air travel and globalised food production is thought to be the cause of 'airport' malaria — namely the recent spread of malaria to areas such as the USA and Europe, particularly in the vicinity of airports, ports and other transport nodes.

As strains of malaria become increasingly resistant to front-line anti-malarial drugs such as chloroquine and SP (sulfadoxine-pyrimethamine), the WHO is encouraging the development and deployment of a new group of anti-malarials based on artemisinin compounds. Artemisinin is a drug derived from the plant *Artemisia annua* that for centuries has been used by the Chinese for the treatment of a range of illnesses, including malaria. Claims are being made that such drugs not only prevent people from contracting malaria, but may in some cases actually cure those who have contracted it. Only time will tell, but maybe artemisinin offers a glimmer of hope.

It is likely that malaria will remain a debilitating and lethal infectious disease until the Anopheles *mosquito has been driven to extinction.*

12 **Using case studies**

Question
Which approach do you think offers a better way of conquering malaria — spraying the breeding areas of the mosquito with regular doses of pesticide or making sure that every child takes a prophylactic?

Guidance
Think in terms of feasibility and costs.

The bottom line to this examination of a range of infectious diseases is a mixed one. Modern medicine has had its triumphs in the form of diseases brought to the brink of extinction by vaccines and drugs. Equally, there remains a hard core of infectious diseases as yet undefeated by medical research. In between, there remain those diseases that break out periodically.

Non-infectious diseases

Given the great diversity of health risks that come under the heading of non-infectious diseases, it would help to group most of them under one of three major headings:

■ Diseases associated with ageing.
■ Lifestyle diseases related to the spectrum running from acute poverty to extreme affluence.
■ Diseases linked to pollution, mainly of air and water.

Diseases associated with ageing

It is an inescapable reality that the longer we live, the more we are confronted with health risks. Those health risks arise from the general deterioration of the human body and mind as we grow older. The challenge posed by such health risks is most evident today in developed countries with their 'greying' populations. Three case studies follow, the first looking at a disease that is exclusive to the male population — prostate cancer. The next two diseases affect men and women alike, and both are recognised as degenerative and genetic disorders. However, the difference between them is that the incidence of cardiovascular disease is known to be increased by lifestyle factors. At present, no lifestyle factors have been identified as contributing to the incidence of Alzheimer's disease.

PROSTATE CANCER

Case study 14

Is it really on the increase?

Prostate cancer is the most common cancer in men in the UK. In 2006, more than 35 000 men in the UK were diagnosed with the disease. The prostate is a gland of the male reproductive system. Over the last 30 years, prostate cancer rates in the UK have almost tripled. But this rise is not to be seen as any sort of 'epidemic'. It simply reflects the fact that our detection of it has greatly improved, largely because of the widespread use of the diagnostic PSA test, which measures the level of prostate specific antigen in a sample of blood.

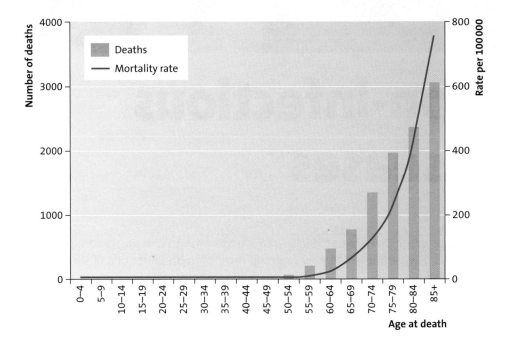

Figure 3.1
Prostate cancer: age-specific deaths and mortality rates in the UK, 2007

So what causes prostate cancer? The short answer is we do not really know. It is very evident that the disease is age-related (Figure 3.1). Over 60% of new prostate cancer cases are diagnosed in men aged over 70. But geographical variations in the incidence of the disease worldwide suggest that there may be other causal factors. For example, the highest rates occur in the USA, Australia, New Zealand, and western and northern Europe. West African men and black men from the Caribbean have a higher risk of prostate cancer than white men. Men born in Asia have a lower risk of prostate cancer than men born in the UK. These facts suggest that there could possibly be lifestyle as well as genetic causal factors.

Although prostate cancer is the most common male cancer in the UK, it is not the biggest killer — lung cancer is. Around 10 000 men die from prostate cancer each year. However, as a result of early diagnosis and new treatments, more and more men are surviving the disease and eventually dying from other causes. The 5-year survival rate is now over 70%.

It is claimed that most men over the age of 60 have prostate cancer. However, thanks to advances in diagnosis and treatment, survival rates are now such that most sufferers will eventually die from some other cause.

13

Using case studies

Write an analysis of the information in Figure 3.1.

Guidance

Age is the key factor. Be sure to compare the trends in the number of age-specific deaths and mortality rates.

ALZHEIMER'S DISEASE

The search for causes

Alzheimer's disease is the most common form of dementia and seems to be on the increase. Dementia affects one in 14 people over the age of 65 and one in six over the age of 80. It is rare for the disease to affect people under 65. There are 820 000 people living with dementia in the UK, a number predicted to reach 1.7 million by 2050.

Alzheimer's is an incurable disease of the brain that attacks the cells, nerves and neurotransmitters. The last of these are chemicals that carry messages to and from the brain. Eventually, the connections among the remaining brain cells begin to be destroyed and so the disease worsens.

The early symptoms of the disease are memory lapses and difficulty in finding the right words. As the disease progresses, sufferers become confused, often forgetting the names of people, places, appointments and recent events. Mood swings are common. The loss of memory and the increasing difficulty of communicating with others often cause great frustration. Eventually, patients become incapable of caring for themselves and need help with all aspects of daily life. For relatives and friends of someone with Alzheimer's this is usually the most harrowing aspect of the disease.

No single factor has so far been identified as a cause of the disease. It is likely that a combination of factors is responsible. These factors include lifestyle, diet and environment, but especially age. It is very clear that the risk of developing Alzheimer's increases with age.

At present, there is no cure for Alzheimer's disease. Some drugs can ease the symptoms and, in some cases, slow down the progress of the disease. Dementia costs the National Health Service (NHS) £17 billion a year, and the economy as a whole, £23 billion. However, only £7.2 million is allocated for dementia research by the Medical Research Council. The Alzheimer's Society estimates that charitable donations towards research into the disease amount to £50 million a year — a tenth of the figure donated to cancer charities in the UK.

In September 2009 news broke that a team of scientists had identified two genes apparently linked to the development of Alzheimer's disease. Strangely, both genes are linked to other functions — one deals with cholesterol and the other with inflammation. As one of the scientists put it, 'The question now is this — if we lower cholesterol and reduce inflammation, do we modify the risk of people getting Alzheimer's disease?' Only time and more research will tell.

Alzheimer's is perhaps the most frightening of all the degenerative diseases associated with ageing. It is a subset of dementia. Its increasing incidence has serious consequences in terms of providing appropriate professional care (Case study 31).

CARDIOVASCULAR DISEASE

Lifestyle and ageing

Cardiovascular diseases are a group of diseases that involve the heart or blood vessels (arteries and veins). The diseases include heart attacks, strokes, high blood pressure and heart failure. Globally, cardiovascular diseases are estimated to account for 30% of all deaths. This makes them the world's number one killer. In 2005 an estimated 17.5 million people died from the diseases. Of these deaths, 7.6 million were due to heart attacks and 5.7 million due to stroke. About 80% of these deaths occurred in low- and middle-income countries. If current trends continue, by 2015 an estimated 20 million people per year will die from cardiovascular diseases (mainly from heart attacks and strokes).

Figure 3.2
The incidence of four cardiovascular diseases, by age and sex

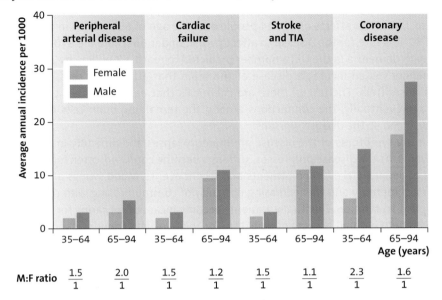

Heart attacks and strokes are caused by a blockage that prevents blood from flowing to the heart or the brain. The most common cause is a build-up of fatty deposits on the inner walls of the blood vessels. The blood vessels become narrower, less flexible and more likely to become blocked by blood clots. When this happens, the blocked vessels cannot supply blood to the heart and brain, which then become damaged. Figure 3.2 shows how the incidence of four types of cardiovascular disease increases with age and that in all four cases and in both age groups, the incidence is higher among males.

Smoking, physical inactivity and an unhealthy diet have long been recognised as major causes of cardiovascular diseases. They do so through the medium of high blood pressure and high levels of cholesterol. (Today, diabetes is recognised as a major risk factor of equal significance. It too is partly related to diet.) So, presumably, the better your lifestyle, the longer it will be before one of the cardiovascular diseases strikes.

The challenging question with this group of diseases is the degree to which their mortality rates can be reduced by lifestyle changes. The fact remains, however, that even people with healthy lifestyles will succumb to these diseases.

14 **Write an account of the incidence of cardiovascular disease based on an analysis of Figure 3.2.**

Guidance

Compare the four diseases in terms of their incidence and male/female differences.

Lifestyle diseases

Alcohol abuse (*Case study 5*), smoking, poor diet and lack of exercise have already been examined as lifestyle factors with serious health risks. Of the four case studies that follow, the first two consider the health risks associated with eating too little and too much. The second two look at the consequences of addictive behaviours with global distributions.

MALNUTRITION IN ETHIOPIA

Case study **17**

A persistent 'epidemic'

With daily calorie intake averaging out at 1540 calories per day per person, around 8 million people out of Ethiopia's total population of 77 million rely on food aid in order to survive. But rising levels of severe acute malnutrition are expected to increase that dependency still further. Those most at risk are children under the age of 5. Infant mortality currently stands at 156 per 1000 live births — one of the highest rates in the world (Figure 3.3).

Figure 3.3
A member of the charity Concern Worldwide weighs a baby at a health centre in Ethiopia

Kim Haughton/Alamy

The factors contributing to this malnutrition 'epidemic' are environmental, demographic and economic:

- Relatively high population densities relative to food resources. The overall population density is 72 persons per km^2.
- Climate variability — farming is highly dependent on the rainy seasons: the main one is from June to September, with a lesser one from February to April. In good years, the latter allows farmers to produce a second crop. In recent years, both seasons have failed to produce sufficient rainfall.
- Widespread poverty, which means that many families simply do not have the means to buy food, particularly during times of crop failure.

- Rising global costs of fuel, fertiliser and staple foods are compounding the problem, especially for the poorest Ethiopians. The price of maize and sorghum has doubled within a year, while the price of wheat has increased by over a half.

Medical conditions caused by the general lack of food (malnutrition) include:
- marasmus — general food deficiency (starvation) resulting in severe weight loss and weakness
- kwashiorkor (protein malnutrition) — bloated stomach
- malnutrition-related diabetes mellitus (MRDM) — a form of diabetes with high sugars, but without causing diabetic ketotic coma

The lack of certain vitamins can cause various medical conditions, even if other aspects of the diet are adequate (see also Table 4.1 on page 54), including:
- scurvy (vitamin C deficiency/ascorbic acid deficiency): immune weakness
- rickets (vitamin D deficiency): weakened bones
- vitamin A deficiency: night blindness
- beriberi — a deficiency in thiamine, vitamin B1
- pellagra — a deficiency in niacin, vitamin B3
- vitamin B12 deficiency
- riboflavin deficiency

Certain minerals are also required in the diet for full health. Lack of minerals can lead to diseases, including:
- goitre — iodine deficiency; swelling of the thyroid gland in the neck
- anaemia — lack of iron, with symptoms such as tiredness and fatigue
- bone weakness due to calcium deficiency

The vulnerability of children to malnutrition is explained by a complex interaction of factors, such as the mother's health and diet during pregnancy and her knowledge of basic nutrition, as well as poor-quality water supply and sewage disposal.

It is difficult to see any long-term solution to this humanitarian crisis in Ethiopia and other areas in the Horn of Africa. Possible actions include large-scale water conservation projects, the development of food production methods, better adaptation of crops and livestock to the increasingly arid conditions, and perhaps population control. The only option in the short term is to rely on food aid provided by the international community and to hope that this will help to stave off the plethora of diseases associated with malnutrition.

Case study 18 — THE OBESITY PANDEMIC

More calories than we need

There have always been fat people, and it has long been known that the incidence of people in a population who are **obese** (with a body mass index [BMI] of more than 30 and **overweight** (BMI >24.9) increases with the general rise in the standard of living. It also increases with age. For example, the number of people in England aged 55–64 who are overweight or obese is more than double the number aged 16–24. However, the alarm bells are being rung in the UK because the percentage of adults who are obese has roughly doubled since the mid-1980s. Calorie intake in the UK has now risen to 3190 per person per day.

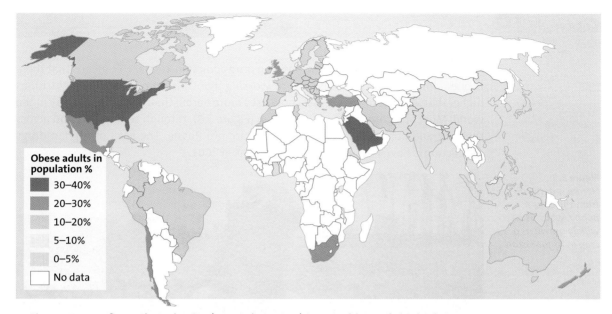

Obese adults in population %
- 30–40%
- 20–30%
- 10–20%
- 5–10%
- 0–5%
- No data

Figure 3.4 confirms that obesity (more than 20%) is a problem of the high-income countries of Europe, North America and Australasia. But it is worth noting that some of the middle-income countries, such as Brazil, Mexico and South Africa, already share the problem. So too do the oil-rich states of the Middle East.

Genetic factors account for a proportion of the obese, but the recent and sudden surge in weight levels (referred to as **globesity** since it is so widespread) can only be explained by environmental factors. Eating too many calories for our energy needs is a cause of the current obesity epidemic. The type of food eaten is also playing an important role. Researchers are discovering that there are a number of disorders resulting from overconsumption of fats and refined white flour combined with a low fibre intake. Increases in the consumption of calorie-rich foods, as evidenced by the growth of fast-food chains and higher consumption of soft drinks, also add to the 'energy surplus' that leads to obesity. The problem is made worse by the small amount of exercise that figures in modern lifestyles; exercise being a potentially effective burner of excess calories.

The outcome of obesity is a range of increased health risks, from Type 2 diabetes to coronary heart disease, from strokes to colon cancer.

Our modern lifestyles are major contributors to the obesity epidemic — we are eating more than we need, our diet includes too much of the wrong foods, and we are taking too little exercise.

Figure 3.4
Globesity

15 Using case studies

Devise a propaganda strategy highlighting the costs of obesity.

Guidance

Focus, of course, on the health risks — diabetes, cardiovascular disease etc. — but also think about other costs, such as the need for special clothing and furniture, and problems with public transport.

Health & Health Risks

Arrest rather than reform

It is estimated that there are now 2 million drug addicts in Russia. This means that there is one addict for every 50 Russians of working age. This ratio is roughly eight times higher than in EU countries. Russia now uses more heroin than any other country in the world. Most of it comes from Afghanistan (Figure 3.5), through central Asia and across the long and porous border with Kazakhstan into Russia. The level of Afghan drugs production is now 44 times higher than it was in 2001.

Figure 3.5
Heroin is derived from the opium poppy, which is widely grown as a crop in Afghanistan

Carol Lee/Alamy

It has been difficult for the Russian government to admit to having such a high incidence of drug addiction. As a result, its attitude towards addicts has been one of identifying and punishing them rather than helping to wean them off drugs. Substitution therapy using methadone is banned in Russia. All this is having disastrous consequences. Most notable is the spread of hepatitis C and HIV/AIDS as addicts share needles and syringes rather than collecting clean ones from exchange points. They worry that if they go to an exchange point they will be arrested and sent to prison.

The reasons for this heroin epidemic are complex, but two factors would seem to be particularly significant:

- The profound changes in Russia that have followed the collapse of the hardline communist regime around 1990. Many people simply have not been able to cope with the transition.
- The easy availability of cheap heroin from Afghanistan.

Whatever the reasons behind this heroin epidemic, more than 30 000 people die from drug use every year, and this in a sparsely populated country with a shrinking population. It is a mortality statistic that Russia cannot afford to ignore.

The current heroin epidemic in Russia appears to be the consequence of easy access to cheap supplies and widespread personal insecurity associated with deep-rooted political change.

MALIGNANT MELANOMA

The deadliest skin cancer

Many of us like to look 'bronzed' and as if we take regular sun-seeking holidays. Acquiring this 'look' is reckoned to raise our feel-good factor. However, more than 10 000 people a year in the UK are developing the deadliest form of skin cancer, thanks to what is increasingly referred to as binge-tanning. This results from an excessive use of sunbeds, either in our homes or in tanning parlours, and from package holidays during which hours are spent sunbathing.

Rates of skin cancers have more than quadrupled in 30 years (Figure 3.6), rising from 3.4 cases per 100 000 people in 1977 to 14.7 per 100 000 in 2006. Since 2003, the UK government has spent more than £420 million on annual campaigns warning us of the dangers of not protecting our bodies from sunlight or UV radiation. But skin cancer remains the most commonly diagnosed cancer in the UK, with 100 000 new cases each year. Figures released in 2009 showed that the number of women in their twenties diagnosed as having melanoma was nearly double the number in the same age bracket diagnosed as having breast cancer. Experts are warning people of all ages to stay away from sunbeds and to use a high-factor sun lotion when outdoors in the sun.

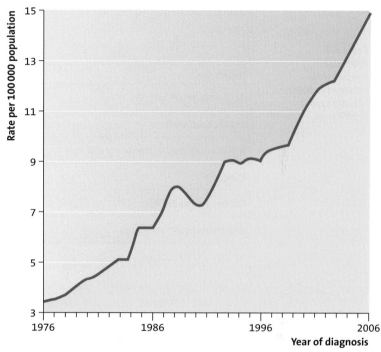

Figure 3.6
The growing problem of malignant melanoma in the UK, 1976–2006

If melanoma is diagnosed early when thin and on the surface of the skin, it can be removed easily. If left, it can spread through the lymph system or the bloodstream. This can be serious and in some cases fatal. Surgery becomes more complex, with longer scars and a requirement for skin grafts.

Malignant melanoma is very much a lifestyle disease. Should we be doing more to discourage the idea that a tan is an essential fashion accessory?

---

16 **Write an essay entitled 'Some health risks are cool'.**

Guidance

Case studies 19 and 20 should provide a good start, but can you think of any other 'fashionable' lifestyle activities with clear health risks?

Using case studies

Diseases linked to pollution

Let us consider briefly the relationship between health risks and the environment. It should already be clear from the case studies in Part 2 that there is a link between certain diseases and aspects of the environment, which can act as a medium either for developing bacteria or for dispersing an infection. Another dimension of the environment–health risk relationship is the fact that human pollution of the environment also generates a rash of diseases. Is this a case of scoring an own goal? It also needs to be pointed out that some of the diseases in this category are infectious.

Table 3.1
Potential relationships between exposure situations and health risks

Health risk	Exposure situations		
	Polluted air	Polluted water	Polluted food
Acute respiratory infections	✔		
Diarrhoeal diseases		✔	✔
Malaria and other vector-borne diseases		✔	✔
Cancer	✔	✔	✔
Cardiovascular disorders	✔		
Chronic respiratory diseases	✔		
Injuries and poisonings	✔	✔	✔

We have already looked at the occurrence of typhoid (*Case study 9*) and cholera (*Case study 12*), both of which are linked to water pollution. *Case study 21* looks at water pollution from a different perspective. *Case studies 22* and *23* illustrate the health risks associated with polluted air.

Case study 21 — CHINA'S POLLUTED RIVERS

Flowing with health risks

China is renowned for its air pollution and associated health risks, but in fact its polluted rivers are an even greater threat to health. All the major rivers of China are being severely polluted by industrial emissions, untreated domestic waste and agricultural runoff. Each year, one-third of industrial wastewater and two-thirds of household sewage are emitted untreated, so it is not surprising that more than 75% of the rivers flowing through Chinese cities are unsuitable for drinking or fishing.

Nearly 700 million people in China lack access to safe water and consume water contaminated with animal and human waste. The resulting high levels of faecal organisms are responsible for spreading a variety of illnesses. These include parasitic flukes and worms, hepatitis A, bacterial dysentery, infectious diarrhoea and typhoid. It is estimated that 190 million people per year suffer from illnesses related to water pollution.

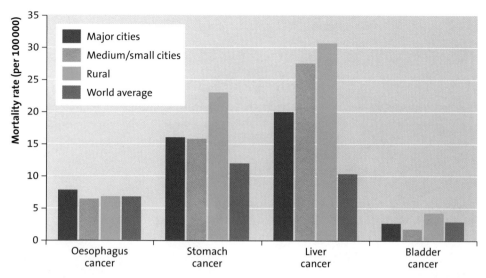

Figure 3.7
Mortality rates for
cancers associated
with water pollution
in China, 2008

Along China's major rivers, particularly the Huai, Hai and Yellow, communities report higher than normal incidences of cancer, tumours, spontaneous abortions and children being born with diminished IQs. All are blamed on the high level of contaminants in the soil and water. For example, it is claimed that the high incidence of stomach, liver and bladder cancers in rural China is associated with the widespread use of industrial wastewater to irrigate farmland. This practice is especially common in the northern regions, where water is scarce. This is well illustrated by the mortality rates shown in Figure 3.7.

China has some of the most polluted rivers in the world, the outcome of two decades of breakneck and largely unrestrained industrial growth. The Chinese government has struggled to balance economic growth with concern about its impacts on human health and the environment. To date, the balance has tipped in favour of the former.

COOKING SMOKE

Case study 22

A silent killer

It is ironic to think that while huge sums of money have funded research into the harmful effects of outdoor air pollution, little has been spent on protecting people from the health risks of indoor air pollution. The one exception has been research into the health risks associated with smoking tobacco. Wood, stubble, dung and grass are used daily in about half the world's households as energy for cooking and heating. In many developing countries they are burnt in open fires or inefficient stoves, in poorly ventilated rooms. The results are an incidence of ill-health and a death rate much higher than those caused by outdoor air pollution.

Particulates and carbon monoxide are among the harmful by-products of burning biomass. Prolonged exposure to these substances can cause serious respiratory infections, as well as pneumonia, tuberculosis and eye cataracts. In contrast, coal smoke contains sulphur and nitrogen oxides as well as hydrocarbons. It is known that exposure to these can lead to cancer.

Picture Contact/Alamy

Figure 3.8
Preparing food on an indoor fire in Kagera, Tanzania

The WHO estimates that about 2500 million people in the world, particularly women and children, are exposed to excessive levels of indoor air pollution. Most of this pollution comes from burning biomass and coal indoors in ovens that are badly designed and lack proper chimneys (Figure 3.8). African countries and India have the worst record for indoor pollution in rural homes, while the record for urban homes is worst in Latin America, India and China.

For most people, home is regarded as a place of safety. The reality is that in many homes smoke is lurking as a silent killer.

Case study 23 — MEXICO CITY

A global pollution hotspot

Mexico City has the distinction of being not only one of the world's largest cities but also one of the most polluted (Figure 3.9). This is the outcome of a number of factors:

- The sheer size of the city — a population of around 20 million may be expected to generate a fair amount of pollution of all types, including light, noise and smell.
- Its economic success — the concentration of many polluting industries unhindered by lax anti-pollution laws.

Figure 3.9
The world's most polluted megacities

Legend:
- Severe
- Heavy
- Moderate
- Low

	Sulphur dioxide	Particulate matter	Lead	Carbon monoxide	Nitrogen dioxide	Ozone
Mexico City						
Buenos Aires						
Beijing						
Cairo						
Seoul						
Karachi						
Jakarta						
Los Angeles and São Paulo						

- A heavy reliance on the motor vehicle — more than 3.5 million vehicles now fill the city streets; 30% of them are more than 20 years old. The most widely used form of public transport is the motor bus.
- The nature of its site — located in the crater of an extinct volcano, Mexico City is about 2240 metres above sea level. The lower atmospheric oxygen levels at this altitude lead to motor vehicle fuels not being completely burnt. This results in higher emissions of carbon monoxide and hydrocarbons. Intense sunlight turns these noxious gases into smog. In turn, the smog prevents the sun from heating the atmosphere enough to penetrate the temperature inversion layer that blankets the city. As a result, for much of the year the city lies shrouded in a dense and deadly smog caused by cold air sinking down into the city, trapping pollution beneath it.

Figure 3.10
The origins of air pollutants in Mexico City

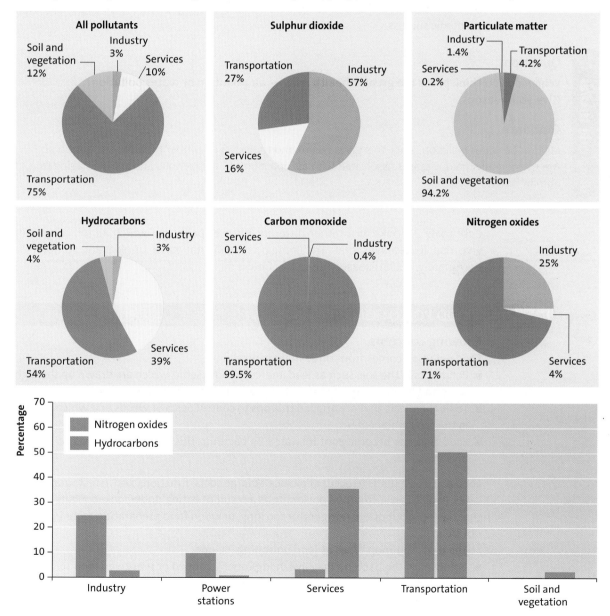

The main source of air pollution is the internal combustion engine (75%), followed by natural sources (12%), services (10%) and industries (3%) (Figure 3.10). Carbon monoxide, nitrogen dioxide and hydrocarbons arise mainly from motor vehicle emissions, while sulphur dioxide is related to industrial activity.

The two most serious pollutants in Mexico City are ozone (produced when nitrogen oxides and organic compounds react in sunlight) and particulates (minute specks of dust that come from various sources, including road and building construction, smoke-belching diesel trucks and buses, forest fires and the burning of refuse in the open air). Both pollutants irritate eyes, aggravate a range of respiratory and cardiovascular diseases, and lead to premature death. Because of its high levels of pollution, Mexico City has the invidious reputation of being 'the most dangerous city in the world for children'. So it looks as if the residents of Mexico City are the victims of the city's economic success.

17 **Question**

Which do you think poses the greater health risks — air pollution or water pollution? Give your reasons.

Guidance

Might it be water pollution, since this gives rise to and transmits a number of infectious diseases? Are the non-infectious diseases associated with air pollution any less serious and less damaging to human health?

Case study 24 looks at a rather different form of pollution, which all too often can give rise to diseases that are contagious and that have unpleasant symptoms. Fortunately, such diseases are rarely fatal.

 *Case study* **24** FOOD POLLUTION

Growing concerns

Food pollution comes from three main sources:

- Pollutants in the soil, such as lead, mercury and arsenic, which are drawn up through roots and become part of plants that are then consumed by humans.
- Toxic chemicals that are applied to crops to control pests or weeds and which remain in the food when eaten.
- Food that has become contaminated by bacteria. This is usually referred to as food poisoning.

Food poisoning tends to occur at picnics, at large social functions and in restaurants and cafés. People can suffer food poisoning as a result of eating undercooked meats or food that has been out of the refrigerator too long, or when food preparation techniques are not clean.

The most common types of food poisoning include:

- botulism — the bacteria may live in improperly canned or preserved food
- *campylobacter* — the most common cause of food poisoning
- cholera — see *Case study 12*

- *E. coli* — this is a large and diverse group of bacteria. Although most strains are harmless, some can cause sickness, some can lead to other illnesses and a few can cause death unless promptly treated. It is the most common cause of travellers' diarrhoea.
- *Listeria*
- *Staphylococcus aureus* — this bacterium can cause infection when a food handler contaminates food products that are served or stored at room or refrigerator temperature.
- *Salmonella* — any food can become contaminated if food preparation conditions and equipment are unsanitary. This is a common type of food poisoning and the cause of most food poisoning deaths.

In England and Wales there were 92 000 reported cases of food poisoning in 2007. The real figure could be much higher, because many people with mild symptoms do not report them. The Food Standards Agency (FSA) estimates that there are around 850 000 cases of food poisoning each year in the UK, and roughly 500 deaths. The potential killers would appear to be *E. coli*, *Listeria* and *Salmonella*.

The best way to prevent food poisoning is to practise good food hygiene. For example, always cook food at the right temperature and wash your hands with soap and warm water after going to the toilet and before and after handling food.

The recurrence of food poisoning is something that should not be happening in a country such as the UK, given our knowledge of food hygiene and the availability of modern cooking and food storage equipment.

Uncertainties

The last two case studies in Part 3 come with a 'health warning' — in other words, we cannot always be certain about causal factors. There is still much to learn. The first carries a warning about jumping to premature conclusions.

LESSONS FROM SELLAFIELD

Case study 25

Tracking down the real causes
It was back in 1984 when the media first drew attention to an unusually large number of cases of childhood leukaemia near the Sellafield nuclear reprocessing plant in west Cumbria. All the children suffering from the disease were born in the nearby village of Seascale. Was the nuclear plant to blame? If so, what were the causal links?

- Some scientists were convinced that the high incidence of leukaemia was a direct result of contamination on nearby beaches. In their view, the radioactivity of Sellafield's outfall into the Irish Sea was to blame.
- Others argued that the exposure to radioactivity occurred through consumption of local seafood and locally produced foodstuffs.
- Still others thought that the causal link was the high radiation doses that the children's fathers received during their work at the Sellafield plant.
- At one time, it was thought by some that the children had caught the disease as babies as a result of crawling on floors that were coated with radioactive dust.

Figure 3.11
The nuclear reprocessing plant at Sellafield

Photoshot Holdings Ltd/Alamy

■ Most recently, a number of scientists have suggested that there is no link at all with the reprocessing plant. Their argument is based on the idea that the leukaemia may be caused by a viral infection rather than by exposure to radioactivity. It has been noted elsewhere in areas of substantial in-migration (as was the case with Sellafield in the late 1950s and early 1960s) that in-migrants often bring 'new' viruses with them. If the local population had no previous exposure to the introduced viruses, they would have been likely to have little or no immunity. In short, the impact of any imported virus can be quite considerable.

This last explanation might be termed the population-mixing hypothesis. It is also well illustrated in *Case study 7*.

In other diseases, the causes are complex and are not yet entirely understood. This has already been illustrated with respect to Alzheimer's disease (*Case study 15*). It is also the case with another common 'mental' disease — schizophrenia (*Case study 26*).

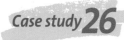

Case study 26 — SCHIZOPHRENIA IN THE UK

Complex causes

Schizophrenia is a common mental illness. It develops in about one in 100 people and can occur in men and women. The most common ages at which it first develops are 15–25 in men and 25–35 in women.

Symptoms include delusions (false ideas), hallucinations (such as hearing voices), disordered thoughts and problems with behaviour. In most cases, the symptoms recur or persist on a long-term basis. Some people have just one episode of symptoms that lasts a few weeks. Treatment includes medication, talking treatments and social support.

The exact cause is not known, but it is thought that the balance of certain brain chemicals (neurotransmitters) is altered. Neurotransmitters are needed to pass messages between brain cells. However, it is not clear why changes occur in the neurotransmitters. Genetic (hereditary) factors are thought to be important.

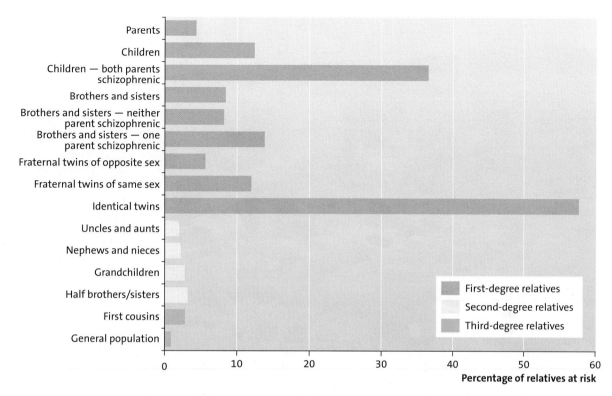

For example, a close family member (child, brother, sister, parent) of someone with schizophrenia has a one in ten chance of also developing the condition (Figure 3.12). This is ten times the normal chance. A child born to a mother and father who both have schizophrenia has a one in two chance of developing it too. However, it looks as if at least one other factor is needed to trigger the condition in people who are genetically disposed to it. There are various theories as to what these factors might be, for example:

- a viral infection during the mother's pregnancy or in early childhood
- a lack of oxygen at the time of birth that may damage a part of the brain
- illegal or 'street' drugs, which may trigger the condition in some people. For example, heavy cannabis users are six times more likely to develop schizophrenia than non-users. Many other drugs, such as amphetamines, cocaine, ketamine and lysergic acid diethylamide (LSD), can trigger a schizophrenia-like illness.

The last case study in Part 3 provides a particularly up-to-date and poignant example drawn from the Iraq War (2003–).

Figure 3.12
The risk of developing schizophrenia

RISING BIRTH DEFECTS IN FALLUJAH

Case study **27**

More war casualties?

The victims of war are not just the military personnel who are killed or injured and their families. So often civilians are caught up in hostilities and they too become victims. An alarming example comes from Iraq — from the town of Fallujah, the scene of much conflict (Figure 3.13). Doctors here report that they are seeing in their surgeries many more infants than normal who are suffering from chronic deformities (particularly in

AFP/Getty Images

Figure 3.13
War-torn Fallujah—doctors here now think there might be a link between the rising number of deformities in infants and the toxic materials used in the conflict

the head and spinal cord) and various cancers. They are beginning to wonder whether there might be a link between these conditions and toxic materials that have been used in the fighting between Sunni and Shia groups or between the Allied forces and the insurgents.

The finger of suspicion is currently pointing towards chemical poisoning or radiation, and in particular to the use of weapons containing white phosphorous. It is known that such weapons were used in the Fallujah area in 2004. However, medical experts say that the high incidence of infant abnormalities may well involve a number of factors. These include air pollution, malnutrition, drug abuse during pregnancy and the stress on pregnant mothers associated with living in a conflict area. As one health official put it, 'We simply don't have the answers yet.'

It is sobering to find that, as yet, there has been no research into the health risks associated with the use of white phosphorous in weapons. Could it be that these abnormal infants are 'next generation victims' of the Iraq war?

18 Using case studies

Question

Explain why it may be dangerous to jump to premature conclusions about the causes of particular diseases.

Guidance

Think in terms of treatment and other remedial actions. A wrong diagnosis of the cause could lead to the wrong treatment. Besides Sellafield, research other incidents such as Chernobyl and Bhopal.

In Part 3, we have looked at a range of diseases, both of the body and of the mind. With the possible exception of food poisoning, all the diseases considered have been of a non-infectious nature. What emerges from the first two categories of disease (degenerative and lifestyle) is that much remains unknown in terms of their causes and causal mechanisms. Finding possible 'cures' to these diseases will have to wait until that causal ignorance is rectified.

Part 4

The impacts of disease

Having sampled some infectious and non-infectious diseases, we should now move on to consider their impacts. While both types of disease have impacts that fall under one of four broad headings, there are some significant differences. The headings are:
- demographic
- social
- economic
- environmental

Demographic

Mortality rates

Mortality rates and life expectancy are two important demographic measures of the effects of disease on populations, and they reflect different impacts of disease. A serious outbreak of disease is likely to boost the mortality rate; if it is chronic and persists for long enough, it might even reduce life expectancy. Mortality rates provide a snapshot of a year's duration. A major epidemic of a fatal and contagious disease would certainly leave its mark on a year's death statistics in a country. But remember that when interpreting mortality rates, it is necessary to take into account the overall age structure of the population (*Case study 28*).

Case study **28** STANDARDISED MORTALITY RATES

A basis for comparison

Medical researchers and geographers frequently want to compare places or populations in terms of their mortality rates. In so doing, however, they need to allow for the fact that one area might have an older population than another. Older people are more likely to die than the young, so the age structure of a population needs to be taken into account. This is done by comparing the age structure of the population of a particular area with that of the country as a whole. This then allows researchers to calculate the death rate that would have been expected had the area's age structure been identical to that of the country as a whole. An index value of 100 indicates that the death rate of a particular area is the same as that for the country as a whole. A value greater than 100 indicates that the death rate of the area is higher than might be expected given its age structure.

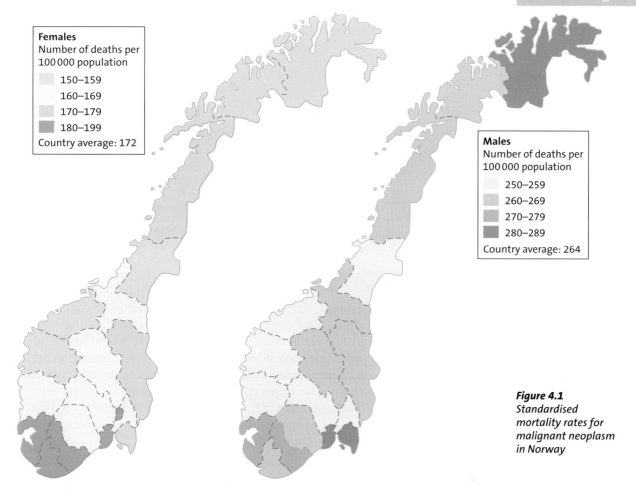

Figure 4.1
*Standardised
mortality rates for
malignant neoplasm
in Norway*

Standardised mortality rates can also be applied to specific causes of death. Figure 4.1 shows the incidence of deaths from malignant neoplasm (a type of cancer) in Norway. Because males and females differ in terms of their susceptibility to particular diseases, the researchers have produced two maps, one for each sex. Such maps allow researchers to home in on areas of particularly high or low incidence. This in turn may be used to track down possible causal factors.

Standardised mortality rates have an important role to play in:
■ *assessing the true significance of particular diseases in terms of mortality*
■ *comparing the incidence of death in different areas*

19 | **Question**
Explain why it is so important in studies of morbidity and mortality to take into account the age structure of a population.

Guidance
Think in terms of age-specific diseases. Figure 4.2 should help.

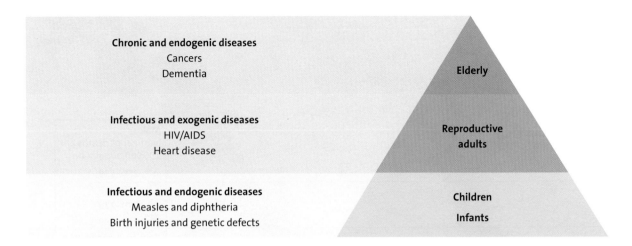

Figure 4.2
Age-related diseases

Many diseases are age-specific in the sense that people within certain broad age ranges typically become their victims. Figure 4.2 tries to illustrate this important point in a very generalised way. Young children are probably the most vulnerable to infectious disease, and this is reflected in infant mortality rates (*Case study 29*). The global infant mortality rate fell by more than 50% during the second half of the twentieth century. Even so, infant mortality continues to erode the base of the age pyramid, but much more so in the case of LICs. There remains a huge gap between the LICs and HICs in terms of this important demographic measure. At present, HIV/AIDS is eating into the age pyramid in the reproductive age range. The very top of the pyramid remains tapered because of the increasing mortality associated with chronic and endogenic diseases that come with advancing age.

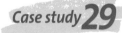 **INFANT MORTALITY**

Killers and causal factors

The infant mortality rate is the number of deaths of children under 1 year old per 1000 live births in the same year. The rate is often used as an indicator of the level of health in a country. In 2009, national infant mortality rates ranged from 180.21/1000 in Angola to 2.31/1000 in Singapore (Figure 4.3). The rates for the UK and the USA were 4.83 and 6.26/1000 respectively.

Traditionally, the most common worldwide cause of infant mortality has been dehydration from diarrhoea. This was particularly the case in LICs. However, the spread of information about how to deal with dehydration by simply drinking a mixture of salts, sugar and water has significantly reduced the number of deaths from this cause. As a consequence, pneumonia is now the number one killer. Other causes include birth defects and SIDS (sudden infant death syndrome). It should also be noted that infants in LICs are especially prone to infectious diseases because of low immunity levels, undernourishment and insanitary living conditions. Sadly, infanticide, child abuse and neglect also contribute to infant mortality.

Two-thirds of deaths before the age of 1 year in the UK are attributed to children being born prematurely or with birth defects, but other social and biological factors can play a role. A recent study has found that babies are most at risk if they are born

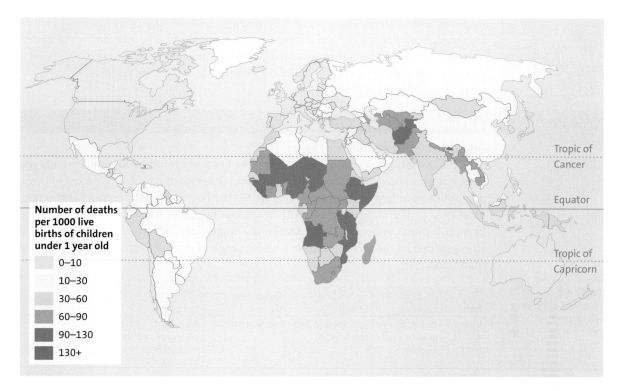

Number of deaths per 1000 live births of children under 1 year old

- 0–10
- 10–30
- 30–60
- 60–90
- 90–130
- 130+

Figure 4.3
Global distribution of infant mortality, 2009

in deprived areas, areas where there is a higher proportion of mothers under 18, and areas with larger ethnic minority populations. The link with poverty is very much as it is in LICs. The amount spent by the NHS on each birth in England is just over £4500, but relatively low infant mortality in some areas was found not to correlate with higher spending on natal services.

Although infant mortality remains commonplace in many developing countries, it persists at a low level in developed countries. There appear to be significant causal differences between these two 'halves' of the world.

Life expectancy

Life expectancy provides a long-term view of a population, and age structure is automatically taken into account. The areas with below-average life expectancy shown in Figure 1.1 (on page 1) are those with substantial health risks, but other areas of the map reflect the more positive outcome of a successful battle against disease, thanks to improving healthcare, medical research and increasing awareness of what constitutes a healthy lifestyle.

Migration

There are many instances where diseases, particularly contagious epidemics, have triggered migrations. Whole settlements infected by the Black Death were abandoned as people sought to escape it (*Case study 6*). There was a mass exodus to the countryside, where lower population densities meant a slowdown in the rate of diffusion of the disease. However, the situation is now very different. Today migrations are rarely, if ever, driven by disease. Instead, the powerful push factors are wars, oppression, natural disasters and starvation. The relationship between disease and migration is now reversed, with migration (including tourism) having a significant impact on the spread and distribution of infectious diseases.

Case study 30 DISEASES OF FAMINE

An added push factor

Over the last 50 years, many migrations have been triggered by famine. Perhaps the most notorious have been those in Ethiopia and the Horn of Africa. While most of these migrations have largely been contained within the boundaries of the country of origin, occasionally they have spilled over into neighbouring states. Although a lack of food has been the prime mover of such temporary migrations, this push factor has been strengthened by the wish to escape a whole range of diseases associated with famine conditions.

Table 4.1
Nutrient-deficiency diseases

Nutrient	Function	Source	Deficiency disease	Symptoms	Scale of disease
Vitamin A	Vision; body growth and healing	Milk, cheese, liver and fish	Xerophthalmia	Poor sight, blindness, reduced resistance to infection	Affects 50% of children in developing world
Vitamin B	Release of energy	Liver, some grains and pulses	Pellagra	Loss of weight, diarrhoea, mental disorder	Prevalent where maize diets are main food
Vitamin B1	Release of energy; nerves	Dried peas and beans, grains, milk and eggs	Beriberi	Loss of appetite, swelling, heart failure	Prevalent where overcooking is common
Vitamin C	Wound healing; iron absorption	Citrus and other fruits, potatoes and green vegetables	Scurvy	Slow healing of wounds, bone weakening	Not known
Vitamin D	Calcium absorption	Sunlight, dairy produce and oily fish	Rickets and osteomalacia	Bone deformities	Prevalent where insufficient exposure to sunlight
Protein	Growth and repair of body tissues	Meat, cheese, eggs, nuts and pulses	Malnutrition — kwashiorkor and marasmus	Muscle wasting and weight loss	Affects about a quarter of the population of the developing world
Iron	Formation of red blood cells	Liver, meat, vegetables with green leaves	Anaemia	Blood disorders causing fatigue and loss of appetite	Affects 917 million people, especially women in the developing world
Iodine	Vital to brain activity	Fish and seafood, eggs, milk and cheese	Stillbirths, endemic cretinism, goitre	Brain damage and mental retardation	600 million people affected

It is only during prolonged famines that the lack of food becomes a direct cause of death. The mortality rate is raised more by people falling victim to diseases related to **undernutrition** and malnutrition. The causal factors are deficiencies in the intake of certain vital nutrients (Table 4.1).

Deficiencies in the intake of specific vitamins and minerals give rise to a range of diseases that differ in terms of their symptoms and severity. Their incidence is much more common and widespread in the developing world.

20 **Using case studies**

Question
What criteria might you use to establish the relative severity of the nutrient deficiencies listed in Table 4.1?

Guidance
You need to think more widely than merely the numbers of people affected.

Social

The potential social impacts of disease involve the complete range from individuals and their families to whole societies, national and international. Disease can be highly disruptive — for example, if a family is deprived of its main breadwinner or a sick family member has to be cared for. At the macro scale, disease creates a demand for healthcare. This obvious impact is explored separately in Part 7, along with the critical issue of access. Disease also creates a demand for education. The more people are informed about disease, its symptoms and causes, the better are the chances of reducing both morbidity and mortality rates.

FAMILIES FACING DEMENTIA
Case study **31**

A challenge for 'greying' populations
Dementia is the loss of mental abilities and most commonly occurs late in life. Of all persons in the UK over the age of 65, between 5% and 8% are demented. This percentage increases considerably with age. Between a quarter and a half of people over 85 are affected. The most common form of dementia, Alzheimer's disease (*Case study 15*), accounts for between half and three-quarters of all cases.

Because of the intensity of care that may be required, it is often difficult for even a loving family to provide all the 'round-the-clock' care that a demented relative may need (Figure 4.4). It is not uncommon for a spouse or children to feel that they are faced with an impossible choice. That is between being utterly overwhelmed (if they try to provide all the care) and feeling they are betraying their relative (if they send them to a nursing home). Local resources to help the care provider include:

Lisa F Young/Fotolia

- respite care
- adult day care
- meals on wheels

Later in the illness, the care needs of the sufferer and their behaviour become such that most are moved to a nursing home for professional round-the-clock care. Family and friends can no longer cope. Unfortunately, the costs of being cared for in a nursing home are very high — frequently in excess of £750 per week. In general, the better-staffed nursing homes cost even more. Another consideration is that a person in the UK only becomes eligible for 'free' caring after all their money has been used up. This means that in the case of a single person all their assets must be liquidated and used to pay for the nursing home expenses. Where there is a surviving spouse, only their home and a limited amount of commonly owned assets will be left. This leaves nothing to reimburse relatives who may have had to bear the costs of caring for that person previously.

The whole situation can easily give rise to guilt feelings on the part of family and friends. First, because they are no longer directly involved in the caring and have to hand over the responsibility to professional carers. Second, because they cannot afford to put their relative or friend in one of the better private nursing homes.

Caring for those with dementia is probably one of the most serious economic, social and emotional challenges confronting the UK and other HICs today. It is likely to be an unceasing problem worldwide.

21 In a group, brainstorm what you think are the more obvious social costs of disease.

Guidance

Think in terms of individuals, families, communities and nations.

Economic

Look back at *Case study 6*, which illustrates the profound economic consequences of the Black Death in the fourteenth century. The impact was truly spectacular. But disease has an even more widespread, persistent and insidious impact on the productivity of labour, as is illustrated in *Case study 32*.

WORKING DAYS LOST	*Case study* **32**

The economic cost of health risks

Chronic diseases in the working population are major contributors to missed work time and lost economic productivity. A recent study in the USA estimated that in the age range 24–54 years, chronic illnesses cause the loss of more than 2.5 billion workdays per year. Although other chronic diseases were more common, cancer had the greatest impact on missed work time. Two-thirds of respondents with cancer had missed 16 workdays in the last month. Workers suffering from ulcers, depression and panic disorders also had high rates of absenteeism from work, as did those with heart diseases or high blood pressure.

These statistics are important to bear in mind in the debate about healthcare in the USA (*Case study 51*). As an American commentator has put it, 'These losses in productivity might be reduced through policies to increase recognition of untreated chronic diseases.' In other words, healthcare should mean an earlier diagnosis of disease, prompter treatment, and an ultimate reduction in the number of working days lost.

Chronic diseases are not the only source of lost working days (Figure 4.5). Two others need to be identified:

- **Work-related illnesses** — in the UK the most commonly reported are musculoskeletal disorders, followed by stress, depression and anxiety. Occupations with an above-average prevalence of the last three include teaching and research professionals, business and public service professionals and corporate managers. These three disorders resulted in an average of 31 days lost per year per case.
- **Industrial injuries** — injuries sustained during the working day resulted in an average of 8 days lost per year per case. It has to be said that thanks to quite strict Health and Safety Executive regulations, the incidence of industrial injuries is relatively low.

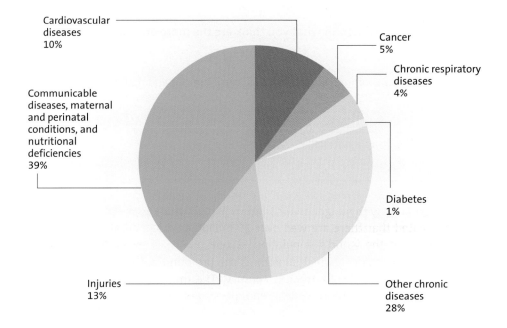

Figure 4.5
Causes of working days lost

Cardiovascular diseases
10%

Cancer
5%

Chronic respiratory diseases
4%

Communicable diseases, maternal and perinatal conditions, and nutritional deficiencies
39%

Diabetes
1%

Injuries
13%

Other chronic diseases
28%

Even so, there are still fatal injuries in the workplace, particularly among those employed in construction and transport. In 2007–08, there were 0.6 fatal injuries per 100 000 workers.

In the UK, these two causes alone accounted for a staggering total of almost 34 million lost working days in 2007–08.

The economic costs of days lost in the workplace resulting from health risks are both considerable and likely to be understated in most countries.

22 **Using case studies**

Make a list of the different ways in which diseases create economic costs. Are the costs any greater or less in LICs compared with HICs?

Guidance

Start with *Case study 32*, but then try to think 'outside the frame' — for example, think in terms of the control and treatment of disease. Are there economic costs in subsistence economies?

Environmental

There is a symbiosis between infectious diseases and the environment. For many of those diseases, the environment acts as a vector — air, water and soil can be both the breeding grounds and the transmitters of infectious disease (see 'Diseases linked to pollution', pages 40–45). And of course, as such diseases are bred and spread, so the environment enters a spiral of decline in terms of increasing health risks and declining ability to retain population. The spiral is well illustrated in the case of so-called **environmental refugees** (*Case study 33*).

ENVIRONMENTAL REFUGEES

A consequence and a cause

Environmental refugees are people who can no longer gain a secure livelihood in their homelands because of drought, soil erosion, desertification or other environmental problems. They are driven not just by a lack of food but also by the wish to escape the diseases associated with hunger and malnutrition (*Case study 30*).

It is estimated that there are well over 25 million environmental refugees today, or nearly 0.5% of the world's population — one person in every 200. This figure compares with a figure of 18 million given for those who are officially recognised as 'refugees' — people who are forced to move for political, religious or ethnic reasons. Many environmental refugee migrations take place within rather than across national frontiers (Figure 4.6). For this reason, they do not hit the headlines very often, which in turn means that they may be seriously underestimated. Migrations across national frontiers are more newsworthy because of the political tensions they so often cause.

While environmental refugees are a response to environmental degradation, the irony is that by migrating and converging on areas still capable of raising food, they set in train the downward path to the very same environmental conditions they have recently escaped. In a word, they create localised overpopulation, and the

Figure 4.6
Ethiopian farmers migrating in search of work and food

Mike Goldwater/Alamy

environmental impacts of this include exhausted soils and polluted and overstretched water resources, as well as the wholesale clearance of trees and bushes to provide much-needed fuelwood. Air also becomes polluted by the dust and the smoke of domestic fires. It is not long before a range of diseases associated with environmental pollution begins to take hold, from cholera and typhoid to diarrhoea and polio.

If present trends continue, the number of environmental refugees could well reach 200 million by 2050 (possibly equivalent to 2% of global population). In short, environmental refugees are fast becoming one of the foremost human crises of our time.

The costs of environmental refugee movements are enormous in terms of the trauma, stress and alienation acutely felt by individual migrants and the environmental impacts of their migrations.

23 **Question**

Explain and illustrate the two-way relationship that exists between disease and the environment.

Guidance

The two strands are: **(1)** how specific environmental conditions nurture particular conditions, and **(2)** how diseases impact on environments in terms of their habitability and attraction to humans.

Using case studies

Across the board

We round off Part 4 with a case study of the HIV/AIDS pandemic, which allows us to see the 'across the board' impacts of this highly infectious and as yet unconquered disease.

Case study 34 THE HIV/AIDS PANDEMIC

Its devastating impacts

Acquired immune deficiency syndrome (AIDS) is an incurable disease that was first identified in 1980. It results from infection by the human immunodeficiency virus (HIV). By gradually destroying the body's defences against disease, it opens up the way for a whole range of opportunistic infections to occur. AIDS is therefore something of an umbrella term to cover all of those infections, one or more of which will ultimately be the cause of death. Examples include pneumonia, malaria and typhoid.

Although HIV is highly infectious, it has a long incubation period of at least 6 years. It is essentially a sexually transmitted disease, but it can be passed on in other ways, such as through contaminated blood or blood products, through contaminated hypodermic needles, and even from mother to child during childbirth.

Since 1980, HIV/AIDS has spread around the globe to warrant the status of a pandemic. It is one of today's 'big killers'. In 2008 it was estimated that 33 million people were HIV-positive and that more than 25 million people had died of AIDS-related diseases since 1981.

Figure 1.5 on page 5 shows the very high incidence of HIV in Africa, particularly in the south. Also catching the eye is the eastern Europe and central Asian region and parts of south and southeast Asia. The impacts of the HIV/AIDS pandemic are most devastating in those parts of the world, and none greater than the direct effects on their populations.

Demographic

It is already clear that the advent of HIV/AIDS has set in motion a chain of demographic events, a vicious downward spiral with the potential to devastate whole populations (Figure 4.7). Initially, HIV/AIDS hit the young adult cohorts of the age pyramid, since the virus is transmitted most vigorously among the sexually active and drug users. More recently, the 'erosion' of the middle sections of the age pyramid has spread in two directions. It has moved up the pyramid for the simple reason that many more people are not surviving into old age. It has also moved down to the base of the pyramid for two separate reasons. First, more and more people are dying while still in their reproductive years. The result is a lowering of the birth rate. Second, there is the very sad fact that before they die, people with AIDS often pass on the HIV to their children. Only a small proportion of those HIV-positive children can expect to live much beyond the age of five. For this reason, the spread of AIDS is both undercutting the base of the age pyramid and boosting rates of infant mortality that are already high because of the general susceptibility of young children to a whole range of diseases (*Case study 29*).

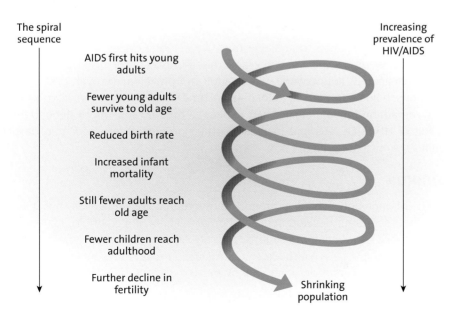

The spiral sequence

AIDS first hits young adults

Fewer young adults survive to old age

Reduced birth rate

Increased infant mortality

Still fewer adults reach old age

Fewer children reach adulthood

Further decline in fertility

Increasing prevalence of HIV/AIDS

Shrinking population

Figure 4.7
The downward spiral of AIDS

Table 4.2
Fact sheet: HIV/AIDS in South Africa, 2007

Total population	47 million
HIV-positive	5.2 million
Prevalence of HIV (national)	11%
Prevalence of HIV (by sex)	Male 7.9% Female 13.6%
Prevalence of HIV (by ethnic group)	African 13.6% White 0.3% Coloured 1.7% Indian 0.3%
HIV-positive babies	Around 70 000 born in 2007
Orphans	1.4 million (at least half due to AIDS)
Life expectancy	54 years (male) 64 years (female) } in 1990 49 years (male) 52 years (female) } in 2007
Birth rate	21/1000 (2000) 18/1000 (2007)
Death rate	13/1000 (2000) 22/1000 (2007)

Table 4.2 gives some indicators of the impact of HIV/AIDS on the population of South Africa.

Social

Reference has already been made to the growing number of children orphaned by HIV/AIDS. Providing for the care of these children is a major challenge, but there are also other social issues. For example, the pandemic is claiming large numbers of teachers, doctors and other service providers. In some countries, notably Malawi and Zambia, healthcare systems have already lost over a quarter of their personnel to the pandemic. Teachers and students are dying or leaving school, reducing both the quality and efficiency of educational services.

AIDS is setting in motion what are termed 'devastating cycles' of impoverishment. People at all income levels are vulnerable to the impact of the disease, but the poor suffer most acutely. In Botswana, where adult HIV prevalence is over 35%, a quarter of all households can expect to lose an income-earner within the next 10 years. Every remaining income-earner can expect to take on four more dependants as a result of HIV/AIDS. A rapid increase in the number of very poor and destitute families is anticipated (Figure 4.8).

Economic

HIV/AIDS is not only having profound demographic consequences, but it is also threatening economic development and human welfare. For example, it is estimated that per capita GDP in half the countries of sub-Saharan Africa is falling by between 0.5% and 1.2% a year as a direct result of AIDS. Estimates show that per capita GDP in heavily infected countries could fall by more than 20% by 2020.

According to a recent report by the UN Food and Agriculture Organization (FAO), 7 million farm workers have died from AIDS-related causes since 1985, and

Imagebroker/Alamy

16 million more are expected to die in the next 15 years. Food production — especially of staple crops — cannot be sustained. The prospects of food shortages and even famine are real. Some 20% of rural families in Burkina Faso are estimated to have reduced their farming and even abandoned their farms altogether because they no longer have the requisite labour. Rural households in Thailand are already seeing their agricultural output shrink by half. In 15% of these cases, children have been removed from school to take care of family members made ill by HIV/AIDS.

The pandemic is also taking its toll in terms of skilled labour and business managers. Recruitment of such personnel is becoming a top priority. At the same time, firms are suffering because the high rates of illness and absenteeism are greatly reducing the general levels of productivity.

Environmental

The most obvious environmental impacts of HIV/AIDS are to be seen in rural areas. Here, in the worst-hit areas, the impact is summed up in one word — 'neglect'. Cropland, pasture and livestock are abandoned as the number of physically able people diminishes. Food insecurity becomes a real issue. The environment also suffers through the deteriorating management of water supply and waste disposal. Settlements are literally dying.

Having read this wholly depressing and very selective account of the diverse impacts of HIV/AIDS, you will be asking what can be done by way of either checking

Figure 4.8
A Botswanan couple infected with HIV is visited by a pastor

the spread of the disease or alleviating some of its worst impacts. There are three possible courses of action:

- Education — about how HIV is spread, and facilitating the use of condoms and new hypodermic needles.
- Anti-retroviral treatment — this consists of drugs that have to be taken every day for the rest of a person's life. The aim of the treatment is to keep the amount of HIV in the body at a low level. This stops any weakening of the immune system and allows it to recover from any damage that HIV might have caused already. This is not a cure, but it can prevent people from becoming ill for many years. There are associated issues of cost and accessibility, particularly in LICs.
- Research — investigating a possible cure. Pharmaceutical companies have already invested a great deal of time and money, but as yet there is no sight of a cure. Hopes were raised in 2009 by an experimental HIV vaccine that in limited trials cut HIV infections by nearly a third.

24

Using case studies

Question

Explain why the impact of HIV/AIDS varies between countries.

Guidance

(1) Identify the specific impacts. **(2)** Factors — morbidity rates, population structure, lifestyles and ability to control spread (education, availability of anti-retroviral drugs). **(3)** Use contrasting countries to exemplify the differential impacts (e.g. Botswana or South Africa versus UK or USA).

Visit: **www.UNAIDS.org** and **www.avert.org**

Health and the global economy

We live in an age of **globalisation**. The countries of the world are becoming increasingly involved in an expanding **global economy**. Through the media of trade, investment and aid, countries are becoming increasingly dependent on each other. People, capital, goods and services are no longer constrained to the degree they once were by national frontiers. Great technological strides in transport and communication have facilitated these international transfers. Information can now be sent around the world within a matter of seconds, people and goods within a matter of hours or days. The net outcome of all this is that the world has become a 'smaller' place — the friction of distance has been significantly reduced. The emergence of the **global village** and global economy has had a number of impacts on health, and indeed on health risks. We will look at three of these — International Health Aid, Pharmaceutical TNCs, and Migration (Figure 5.1).

Figure 5.1
Health and the global economy

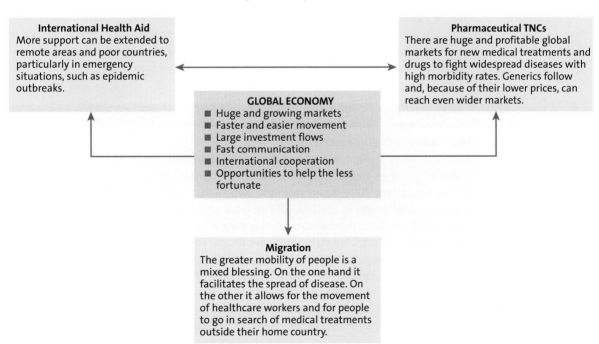

International Health Aid
More support can be extended to remote areas and poor countries, particularly in emergency situations, such as epidemic outbreaks.

Pharmaceutical TNCs
There are huge and profitable global markets for new medical treatments and drugs to fight widespread diseases with high morbidity rates. Generics follow and, because of their lower prices, can reach even wider markets.

GLOBAL ECONOMY
- Huge and growing markets
- Faster and easier movement
- Large investment flows
- Fast communication
- International cooperation
- Opportunities to help the less fortunate

Migration
The greater mobility of people is a mixed blessing. On the one hand it facilitates the spread of disease. On the other it allows for the movement of healthcare workers and for people to go in search of medical treatments outside their home country.

Pharmaceutical TNCs and generics

Of all the players in the global economy, the transnational corporations (TNCs) are among the most influential. Thanks to advances in transport and communication, TNCs are able to set up businesses in virtually any part of the world where there is some economic advantage to be gained, be it cheap labour, cheap raw materials or new markets. TNCs are renowned not just for the geographical spread of their operations but also for the breadth of their business interests. However, within the global community of TNCs there is a fairly conspicuous grouping focused on a relatively narrow range of activities collectively referred to as **pharmaceuticals**. These companies flourish thanks to the fact that health is a major global concern and that the treatment of health risks is a global need. In short, there are huge opportunities to be exploited in satisfying these concerns and needs. To tap into the markets associated with these opportunities, a TNC needs to invest heavily in **research and development (R&D)** and to come up with a new drug or treatment for specific health risks. The more widespread the distribution of a particular risk is and the higher its morbidity, the greater the potential profits.

The R&D associated with the search for new drugs and treatments is usually undertaken in developed countries, often on science parks with university links. Once a new drug has been developed, it is patented and then subjected to clinical trials. If those trials are successful in terms of efficacy and safety, then an application will be made for the drug to be used as an approved medication. Once that approval has been given, attention turns to setting up the necessary production units. How many units will be needed to service the forecast demand? Where best to locate them? The drug is then ready to be launched on the global market and the company can finally begin to recoup the vast sums of money spent on R&D.

 **Case study 35** | THE TOP-TEN PHARMACEUTICAL COMPANIES

Healthcare is big business

Table 5.1 shows the top-ten pharmaceutical corporations in 2008. The USA is home to four of these — indeed 20 of the world's top 50 pharmaceutical companies have their headquarters there. Apart from the two shown in the table, the UK has only one other company (Shire) in the top 50. The table also confirms how very guarded these pharmaceutical companies are about revealing how much they are spending on R&D. It is this that produces breakthrough new drugs. There is much competition, so there is always immense pressure to have a new drug patented. Then follow medical trials, and if these are successful the drug will be approved for prescription to patients. Speed and secrecy are essential if a company is to keep ahead of its competitors and be first in the marketplace. It is this that ensures the profits that such companies need to pay out in dividends to investors and re-invest in the next round of research. R&D is incredibly expensive, and there is always the risk that much time and money can be wasted on dead-end research.

Contemporary Case Studies

Rank by revenue	Company	HQ country	Total revenue (US$ million)	Healthcare R&D (US$ million)	Employees
1	Pfizer	USA	71130	11318	137127
2	Johnson & Johnson	USA	63747	No data	119200
3	Bayer	Germany	48149	3770	108600
4	Hoffmann–La Roche	Switzerland	43970	No data	78604
5	Novartis	Switzerland	41460	No data	98200
6	GlaxoSmithKline	UK	40424	6373	103483
7	Sanofi-Aventis	France	40328	No data	99495
8	AstraZeneca	UK/Sweden	31601	No data	67400
9	Abbott Laboratories	USA	29527	2688	68697
10	Merck & Co	USA	23850	4678	74372

Table 5.1
The top-ten pharmaceutical companies, 2008

Remember that the table shows only the top-ten pharmaceutical companies. There are many others playing an important part in the industry.

25 **Research Shire, a smaller pharmaceutical TNC based in the UK, and produce a short report that takes into account its main activities and the locations in which it operates.**

Using case studies

Guidance

Visit: **www.shire.com** and keep your report for reference when you read about international providers in Part 7.

Once a new drug has been launched on the global market and is doing well in terms of sales, other companies may begin to take an interest. **Generic** drugs are copies of brand-name drugs produced when the patent taken out by the original drug producer runs out. A generic must contain the same active ingredients as the original formulation and should be identical in terms of strength, dosage, administration and safety. For example, Viagra, which was developed by Pfizer, is now widely produced in generic form under such names as Sildenafil and Tadalafil. Not only that, but companies have developed slightly different drugs, such as Cialis and Levitra, that also treat sexual dysfunction.

The advantage of a generic drug is that it is considerably cheaper than the original drug. The principal reason for the relatively low price is that competition increases among generic producers when successful drugs are no longer protected by patents. Companies incur fewer costs in creating the generic drug, and are therefore able to maintain profitability at a lower cost to consumers. Generic manufacturers do not incur the cost of drug R&D, and instead are able to reverse-engineer known drug compounds to allow them to manufacture bio-equivalent versions. Generic manufacturers also do not bear the burden of proving the safety and efficacy of the drugs through clinical trials, since these have already been conducted by the brand-name company. There are, however, concerns about generics, Do they always follow the original formulations exactly? Or are the formulations changed to make drugs simpler and cheaper to produce? Any such changes could, of course, easily affect the efficacy of the drug.

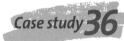

Case study 36 — BANGALORE

Generics galore

Bangalore (population 5.3 million) in central southern India is renowned as an attractive city in which to live and work, thanks to its many gardens and pleasant climate. In the 1980s Bangalore became the location for the first major foreign investment in high technology in India (Texas Instruments). Its residential attractiveness and the cheapness of its well-educated labour have since drawn other TNCs to the city. As a consequence, during the 1990s Bangalore became India's most important centre for a number of industries, including biotechnology, aerospace and information technology. It is now recognised as the IT hub of India and often described as the Garden City. Recently, Bangalore has begun to emerge as a global player in the world of pharmaceuticals. Although some of the world's leading pharmaceutical companies, including AstraZeneca, have a presence in the city, it is building its reputation as a manufacturer of **generics**.

India's top generic maker, Cipla, has its main manufacturing facility in Bangalore. It has been a major producer of generic Viagra and also produced Tamiflu, an antiviral drug to be used for protection against swine flu (*Case studies 38 and 57*). But there are many other generic companies here. The costs of the generic drugs produced are so low that many LICs can afford them. For this reason, Bangalore has become an important node in the 'globalisation' of generic medicines and the global fight against disease. Producing cheaper versions of the latest drugs offers hope in the fight against HIV/AIDS in the less developed parts of the world. It is small wonder that Bangalore is now the third largest and the fastest-growing major metropolis in India.

Bangalore has the reputation of being the generic drug capital of the world. Its rise to prominence illustrates the significance of chance events and non-economic factors.

The pharmaceutical companies are among the beneficiaries of the global economy. They are capitalising and thriving on providing treatments for a diversity of health risks in a fast-growing global population. Many of these risks have global distributions; they vary in terms of the degree to which they are life-threatening. Behind the pharmaceutical TNCs are the opportunistic companies that produce generic copies of drugs that are in particularly great demand. In short, there is much money to be made in medications in this age of the global economy.

26 Question

Examine the arguments for and against the use of generics.

Guidance

On the positive side, think of the benefits of relative cheapness and access. On the negative side, think of possible risks associated with their use.

Contemporary Case Studies

International health aid

While the growth of the global economy has produced great opportunities for companies to produce drugs for the treatment of the global sick, it has also made it much easier for organisations (governmental and non-governmental) to provide healthcare for the sick in particularly poor countries. Information about emergency situations is quickly transmitted, while modern transport makes possible a speedy delivery of international health aid.

INTERNATIONAL HEALTH AID

Case study 37

Meeting emergencies and the dearth of healthcare

As the global economy has grown, so too has the amount of health aid given by HICs to mainly LICs. Not only has the amount of aid increased, but thanks to modern transport and communications, so too has its spatial distribution. Even the populations of the most inaccessible poor areas are beginning to benefit. It is estimated that aid from international health organisations pays for less than 5% of the total healthcare costs of the developing world. However, such organisations do much more than provide funding for healthcare projects. Figure 5.2 shows the various ways and forms in which they deliver health aid.

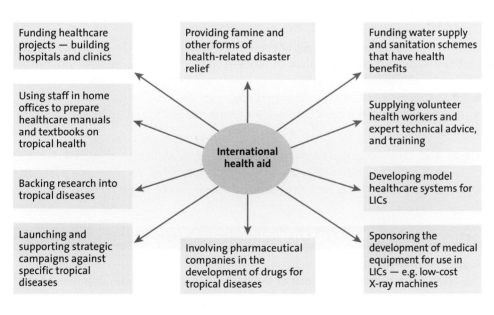

Funding healthcare projects — building hospitals and clinics

Providing famine and other forms of health-related disaster relief

Funding water supply and sanitation schemes that have health benefits

Using staff in home offices to prepare healthcare manuals and textbooks on tropical health

Supplying volunteer health workers and expert technical advice, and training

Backing research into tropical diseases

International health aid

Developing model healthcare systems for LICs

Launching and supporting strategic campaigns against specific tropical diseases

Involving pharmaceutical companies in the development of drugs for tropical diseases

Sponsoring the development of medical equipment for use in LICs — e.g. low-cost X-ray machines

Figure 5.2
Forms of international health aid

There are three main types of organisation providing international health aid:
- **multilateral** — for example, the WHO (*Case study 52*)
- **bilateral** — for example, the United States Agency for International Development (USAID)
- non-governmental or voluntary — for example, Médecins Sans Frontières (*Case study 53*)

It is important to note that in the very poorest countries, the percentage of healthcare costs donated by the developed world is considerably greater than the 5% average. According to the World Bank, in sub-Saharan Africa (excluding South Africa) aid from donor countries averages 20% of total health expenditure, and for five countries — Burundi, Chad, Guinea-Bissau, Mozambique and Tanzania — donor aid pays for more than 50% of the total health bill.

International health aid is delivered by a mix of governmental and non-governmental agencies. It is also delivered by means of two main types of arrangement — multilateral and bilateral.

27 Question

Explain the difference between 'multilateral' and 'bilateral' aid and give examples of each within the realms of healthcare.

Guidance

Check the websites of the WHO and USAID: **www.who.int** and **www.usaid.gov**

Using case studies

Migration

One of the most obvious features of economic globalisation is the greatly increased mobility of people, thanks mainly to modern means of transport. The three main movers of people are:

- the search for work (economic migration)
- the transaction of business between locations, domestic and international
- leisure and recreation (tourism)

These and other population movements have the ability to spread infectious diseases at an incredible speed over considerable distances. Air travel is a particular villain of the piece. This is well illustrated by the spread of swine flu (*Case study 38*).

 Case study 38 | THE 2009 SWINE FLU PANDEMIC

A spectacular diffusion

The H1N1 form of swine flu is one of the descendants of the strain of influenza that caused the 1918–19 flu pandemic, referred to as Spanish flu. As well as persisting in pigs, the descendants of the 1918 virus have continued to circulate among humans ever since, contributing to the normal seasonal epidemics of influenza. Although direct transmission from pigs to humans is very rare, the retention of influenza strains in pigs after these strains have disappeared from the human population might make pigs a reservoir where influenza viruses can persist, later emerging to re-infect humans once human immunity to these strains has waned.

The illness is generally mild, except in some cases for people in higher risk groups, such as pregnant women and people suffering from asthma, diabetes, heart disease or a weakened immune system. The virus spreads via coughing, sneezing or touching contaminated surfaces and then touching the nose or mouth. Symptoms, which last up to a week, are similar to those of seasonal flu, and can include fever, sneezing, sore throat, cough, headache, and muscle or joint pains. To avoid spreading the infection, it was recommended that those with symptoms stay at home from school, work and crowded situations, such as concerts and sports fixtures.

The 2009 outbreak of swine flu was first identified in Mexico City on 19 March. Within 4 months, the outbreak had become a pandemic involving 180 000 cases scattered literally across the globe (Figure 5.3). The speed of its diffusion can only be explained by the speed of modern transport and the huge volume of global passenger traffic. It really needed only one carrier of the virus to fly from Mexico City to, say, London for the virus to be quickly transmitted to and through a high-density urban population. This would happen, for example, at work, at school, in the supermarket or on public transport.

By October 2009, the swine flu pandemic had caused around 4500 deaths. By comparison with the 1918–19 outbreak, the 2009 swine flu was of little consequence. The earlier pandemic was highly lethal and was believed to be responsible for up to 100 million deaths worldwide. The great majority of deaths were the result of secondary bacterial pneumonia. The influenza virus damaged the lining of the bronchial tubes and lungs of victims, allowing common bacteria from the nose and throat to infect their lungs. Nonetheless, in the face of the threatened swine flu pandemic health authorities throughout the world were more than anxious to embark on large-scale vaccination programmes — just in case the H1N1 virus mutated and turned really

Figure 5.3
Spread of swine flu in 2009

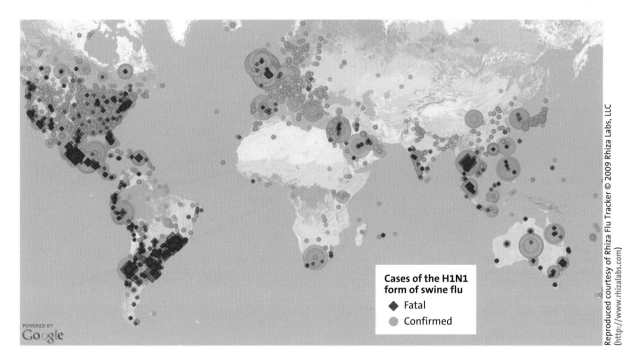

Cases of the H1N1 form of swine flu
◆ Fatal
⬤ Confirmed

nasty. See *Case study 57* for more information about the ways in which governments and business prepared for this possibility.

The 2009 outbreak of swine flu is interesting in that this contagious disease quickly reached the status of a pandemic (thanks to international movement of people) and yet it affected relatively few people, and still fewer cases proved either serious or fatal.

Perhaps some of the migrants responsible for transmitting swine flu were themselves workers in the healthcare industry. They too would be taking advantage of the access to foreign employment opportunities created by economic globalisation. The next case study is just a microcosm of the global market for employment in health.

HEALTHCARE WORKERS HEADING FOR THE UK

It's an ill wind...

Both the NHS and the private medical sector in the UK are relying increasingly upon the services provided by foreign workers. This case study looks at just three types of healthcare migrant.

Locums from the EU

A locum is a doctor who covers for a regular doctor when that doctor is absent, or when a medical practice or hospital is short-staffed. The use of locums in the UK has increased significantly, since most regular doctors no longer work nights or at weekends. Today, the NHS has, on average, 3500 locum doctors working in hospitals on any given day, while there are another 6000 covering GPs. Most of the locum hospital doctors are supplied by private agencies. On the other hand, most GP locums are self-employed, and since no agency fee is involved they are able to offer their services at competitive

Figure 5.4
The movement of healthcare workers into and out of the UK

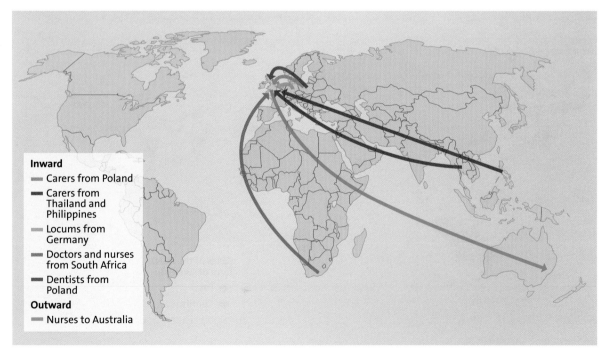

Inward
- Carers from Poland
- Carers from Thailand and Philippines
- Locums from Germany
- Doctors and nurses from South Africa
- Dentists from Poland

Outward
- Nurses to Australia

rates. More than 5000 of the locums currently in the UK come from former Eastern bloc countries.

A row erupted in 2009 over the competency of foreign locums after an outspoken consultant claimed that some of them are clueless about what is expected of them by the NHS. The issue was raised with the European Commission following the case of a German doctor whose patient died after he gave him an overdose of a painkiller on his first UK weekend shift as a locum GP. Clearly, there are risks associated with the use of foreign locums, due to language difficulties and differences in both medical training and practices.

Doctors and nurses from South Africa

The advantage of recruiting doctors and nurses from South Africa is that there are no language difficulties and the professional training is very similar in both countries. Since the 1990s the NHS has successfully recruited large numbers of staff from South Africa. Doctors and nurses have been more than willing to make the move because of concerns about personal security and because of relatively low salaries. As far as is known, those workers have fitted in well in both our hospitals and general practices. However, this migration has had a downside. South Africa has been seriously drained of its medical professionals to the extent that the very existence of its healthcare systems has been threatened. In 2003, 5880 health and medical personnel from South Africa registered in the UK. In that same year, the governments of the UK and South Africa were forced to draw up an agreement restricting the number of workers entering the UK. Underlying that agreement was the recognition that the UK should not be poaching qualified

Figure 5.5
Since the 1990s, the NHS has recruited large numbers of staff from South Africa — as far as is known these workers have fitted in well in both hospitals and general practices

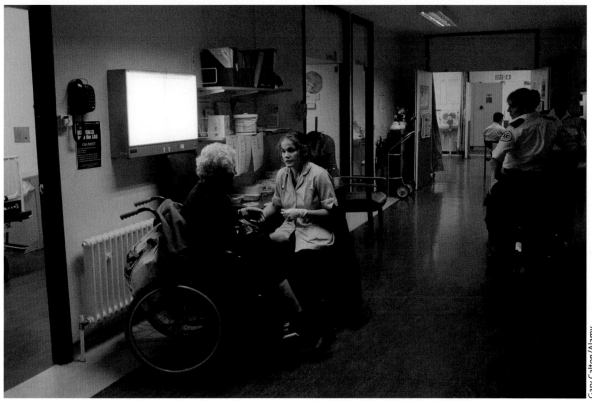

Gary Calton/Alamy

medical staff from a less developed country faced by a number of serious health risks, the most significant being a very high HIV/AIDS morbidity rate.

Care assistants from Poland

A shortage of care workers in the UK has prompted charities and local authorities to turn to Poland to recruit staff for their elderly care homes. Since EU borders opened up in May 2004 to include another ten countries, there have been enhanced opportunities for both workers in those new member states and UK employers. After years of finding it difficult to recruit suitable UK staff, a certain amount of campaigning in Poland soon resulted in an inward flow of young carers. In the main, our care homes have been pleased with their Polish recruits. They are well qualified, have a strong work ethic and are sensitive to the needs of the elderly. There is a downside to this particular healthcare migration. Many of the workers are temporary economic migrants. They intend to return home to Poland after a few years. The return of care workers is beginning to gather pace, since rates of pay are low and there are more and better jobs to be had back home as the Polish economy picks up. In addition, some care homes have been guilty of exploiting and abusing the rights of these workers.

The UK's sick and elderly are generally the beneficiaries of this influx of foreign health workers. However, there are some risks that are to do with language and levels of qualification. But the most serious concern is that the arrival of these workers in the UK is depriving other countries of their skills.

28 **Research the outflows of healthcare workers from the UK in terms of their destinations and the particular skills involved.**

Guidance

You might prepare a global map that complements Figure 5.4. The skill categories might be: surgeons and consultants; nurses; care workers; administrators.

Case study 37 was about aid organisations distributing healthcare to needy parts of the world. The next case study illustrates almost the opposite situation of people going in search of medical treatment in a foreign country, perhaps because that country offers treatment that is prompter, cheaper or of a higher quality than can be obtained at home. The desire for non-urgent cosmetic surgery is a common driving force.

Case study 40 — MEDICAL TOURISM

Travel in search of health

Medical tourism (also known as medical travel or global healthcare) is a term used by travel agencies and the mass media to describe the rapidly growing practice of travelling across international boundaries to obtain healthcare.

Each year, long NHS hospital waiting lists and the high cost of private medicine are persuading around 100 000 UK citizens to become medical tourists. They go abroad for a variety of treatments — infertility, dental, cosmetic and orthopaedic. Orthopaedic treatment includes such things as hip and knee replacements. The costs of a hip replacement in ten countries are shown in Table 5.2. Given the £8000 cost of private treatment in the UK, much money can be saved by having the operation abroad. Even allowing for the costs of travel and a week's accommodation, there are still great savings to be made on the total package. Notice that not all medical tourism destinations are in HICs — India, Malaysia and Tunisia are all popular, for example.

Table 5.2 *A comparison of the costs of having a hip replacement, 2007*

Country	Treatment price	Treatment saving	Package saving
Bulgaria	£2000	87%	69%
Cyprus	£4100	49%	43%
France	£5689	29%	23%
Germany	£5296	34%	26%
Hungary	£4450	44%	40%
India	£3547	56%	49%
Malaysia	£2205	72%	60%
Tunisia	£3000	63%	56%
Turkey	£4725	41%	36%
UK	£8000	—	—

Over 50 countries have identified medical tourism as a national industry. However, **accreditation** and other measures of quality vary widely across the globe, and there are risks and ethical issues that make this method of accessing medical care controversial. Also, some destinations may become hazardous or even dangerous for medical tourists to contemplate.

It is perhaps worth noting that in Cuba medical tourism is a state activity. Medical treatments are traded in exchange for resources that the country needs. For example, an intergovernmental agreement allows people from Venezuela to be treated in exchange for oil.

The greater mobility of people encouraged by modern transport may be responsible for the more rapid spread of contagious disease (Case study 38), but it does have an upside. It allows people, at least those with money, to seek healthcare in foreign countries, but strictly within the private sector.

29

Using case studies

Produce a two-column table that identifies the benefits and costs of medical tourism.

Guidance

Think first in terms of the benefits and risks to the patient, then broaden your thinking to consider possible social and ethical issues.

The global downturn

A booming global economy has encouraged the expansion of pharmaceutical companies, international healthcare aid and medical tourism. However, what have been the impacts of the more recent downturn (the so-called **credit crunch**) on health and health risks around the world? Perhaps the reduction in migration volumes (for example, of business trips and tourism) has put a brake on the speed with which diseases are spread from one country to another. Have the pharmaceutical companies had to reduce their R&D and levels of production, close factories and make staff redundant? The next case study looks at just one, perhaps unsuspected side-effect in the poorer parts of the developing world.

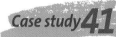

THE CREDIT CRUNCH KILLS

A side-effect of the global downturn
The global downturn of 2008–09 arguably hit the developed world rather harder than the developing world, what with the crashing of banks, the loss of savings and jobs, houses repossessed and so on. However, in 2009 the head of the WHO warned that the poorer parts of the developing world were also experiencing a particularly painful

Figure 5.6
The 'credit crunch'

"YOUR HEALTH AND PENSION BENEFITS WILL REMAIN INTACT, BUT WE HAVE ELIMINATED YOUR SALARY."

backlash. This took the form of a marked increase in female and infant mortality rates. The reasons for this were as follows:

- The credit crunch was reducing the willingness and/or ability of the high-income countries to make donations in support of aid programmes, such as those aimed at improving maternal care and cutting infant mortality rates in the developing world.

- In many parts of the developing world, there is a heavy reliance on **remittances**. This is money sent back home to their families by migrant workers in the developed world. Remittances were declining significantly, as these migrant workers were facing unemployment or a cut in working hours and wages. Normally, much of that money is spent on food, so when the supply of money and food runs out, the risks of malnutrition are increased. Malnutrition is particularly lethal for mothers and their babies.

This case study illustrates the nature of the global village, with its links and interconnections.

Part 5 has aimed to illustrate a few of the ways in which health and health risks are linked to the global economy. While that economy booms, there is the prospect of a general increase in health and the quality of healthcare, as pharmaceutical companies produce new and better treatments and international aid organisations lead the fight against disease and help the most needy parts of the world. However, when that economy falters, it is the people in those same parts of the world whose health suffers most.

30 · *Using case studies*

Discuss with your fellow students other possible ways in which the global recession might have had an impact on health and health risks.

Guidance

You might distinguish between **(1)** the developing and developed worlds and **(2)** infectious and non-infectious diseases.

6

UK health check

Part 6 narrows the spatial focus and tries to answer a basic question — how healthy is the UK's population? Are we right in thinking that the people of an affluent country such as the UK will generally enjoy good health and be relatively free from health risks? In short, we need to undertake a form of health check looking particularly at infectious and lifestyle diseases as well as morbidity rates.

Infectious diseases

Health risks that confront the UK today are largely of the non-infectious kind. Thanks to immunisation and vaccination, most serious infectious diseases have been eradicated (*Case studies 8* and *9*). Table 6.1 shows the schedule recommended for children. These diseases have been virtually eliminated in the UK, but if this situation is to be maintained it is essential that all children complete the schedule (*Case study 11*). Should we make this compulsory for school entry, as in the USA?

At the other end of the age range, given that the country is still prone to annual outbreaks of influenza, all adults over the age of 60 years are encouraged to have a flu jab in the autumn. Swine flu posed a threat to the nation's health (see *Case studies 38* and *57*). In the middle age ranges, we should remember that HIV/AIDS continues to pose a lethal threat.

Table 6.1
UK schedule of recommended vaccines

Vaccine	Age
Diphtheria, tetanus, meningococcal conjugate and polio	First dose — 2 months Second dose — 3 months Third dose — 4 months
Measles, mumps and rubella (MMR)	12–15 months
Booster diphtheria, tetanus, pertussis, polio and second dose MMR	3–5 years
Tuberculosis	10–14 years

31

Using case studies

Research and produce a short report entitled 'The risk of dying from HIV/AIDS in the UK'.

Guidance

Visit: **www.avert.org**

Focus particularly on morbidity rates, their trends and spatial variations.

Non-infectious diseases

However, the UK does not emerge too well from this health check when it comes to non-contagious diseases. It is accepted that with an ageing population, the incidence of such health risks may be expected to increase. Old age, of itself, is not a disease, but it does raise a number of challenges and issues.

OLD AGE IS NOT A DISEASE

Case study 42

Dependency is the problem

There are increasing numbers of elderly people in the UK. People over the age of 65 now account for just over 15% of the population. Many of these pensioners have no problems, but there is an increasing risk of dependency.

The main reasons for this are as follows:

■ Sickness — the health of old people is often poor, not simply because of old age but also because diet, housing, occupation and lifestyle in previous times have not been conducive to good health.

■ Physical disability — at least a third of people over 75, and probably more, can be classified as 'disabled'. The single most common cause of disability seems to be arthritis; the main single reason for ill-health is probably smoking.

■ Dementia — this is believed to affect about 5% of the elderly population (*Case studies 15* and *31*). There are 700 000 people living with dementia in the UK today, a number forecast to double within a generation.

Figure 6.1
Many elderly people have no problems, but there is an increasing risk of dependency

deanm1974/Fotolia

- Poverty — the incidence of poverty among the elderly is relatively high. Unless there is family support, poverty very often means heavy dependence on what the state can provide.

In general, the older a person is, the more likely these problems are to occur.
Other problems associated with old age may include:
- isolation, as family units break up and friends and relatives die or move away
- bereavement, when spouses die
- housing — old people often live in older housing, which may be deteriorating from lack of maintenance
- the problems of obtaining carers — many old people are looked after by women who are themselves ageing

A Green Paper published in July 2009 focused on this growing issue of dependency and paying for the necessary care. The government admits that there will be many more elderly people to look after, and no more money to do so. It also wants people to realise that unless they are very poor indeed, they will have to pay some of their care costs themselves.

The government has already ruled out increasing National Insurance contributions to pay for this social care. The argument is that it would place too much of a burden on the working population. Instead it wants to set up a 'national care service' and sets out three possible ways of funding it:
- A *partnership* approach that shares costs between the individual and the state. The state promises to pay for one-third of the basic costs, no matter what the individual's financial situation is, unless it is dire.
- An *insurance* approach that would enable people to choose to take out protection against the risk of having high care costs. This would reduce the commitment to pay two-thirds of the costs.
- A *comprehensive* approach in which everyone who could afford it would be required to pay into a fund and would get free care and support in return.

There would be a range of ways in which people could pay their contributions in the insurance and comprehensive options.

It is an inescapable biological fact that as people age they become more prone to sickness, physical disability and mental impairment. The best that can be hoped for is to find ways of delaying the onset of these conditions as much as possible and providing suitable healthcare.

32 Question

Examine the reasons why (1) the incidence of poverty is relatively high among the elderly, and (2) a relatively high incidence of disease is often associated with poverty among the elderly.

Guidance

(1) Start by thinking about pensions and income.
(2) Look back at *Case studies 2* and *3*, and reread *Case study 42*.

Lifestyle diseases

While the population of the UK becomes progressively older, the actual morbidity rates of the disabilities associated with old age remain fairly stable. This is attributable to better care and better awareness of the causes of many of those disabilities. However, there are some diseases that are definitely showing a rising incidence in the other age groups of the population. These diseases and their increasing morbidity and mortality are linked to aspects of our modern lifestyle — our diet, our lack of exercise, our drinking habits and our general pace of living. The next three case studies look at the main affluence and lifestyle diseases. It would be helpful to refer to the epidemiological transition in Part 1 (pages 11–12).

OBESITY IN THE UK

Case study **43**

Identifying the heavyweight parts of the country

A survey undertaken in 2006 based on GPs' assessments of their patients shows that almost one in four adults is obese and that the rates are rising. According to the overall incidence of obesity in adults and children, Shetland, Orkney, the Outer Hebrides, Wales and parts of the Midlands and northern England are Britain's obesity hotspots (Figure 6.2). What is also interesting is that the map hints that the incidence of obesity seems to be almost inversely proportional to levels of affluence.

Not only are we eating too much, putting on weight and placing an unnecessary strain on our hearts, we are also eating too much of the wrong things, such as dairy products, meat, sugar and fast foods. These tend to clog the blood circulation system. In short, many of us are taking considerable health risks, which are likely to lead to premature death from heart disease, diabetes or some forms of cancer.

An increasing incidence of obese and overweight people is something that the UK shares with other parts of the world (Case study 18). The associated health risks are no less here than elsewhere.

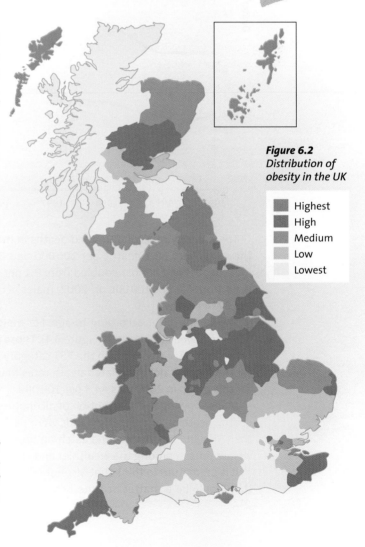

Figure 6.2
Distribution of obesity in the UK

Highest
High
Medium
Low
Lowest

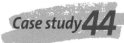

ALCOHOL-RELATED DEATHS IN THE UK

Good and bad news

Following rapid increases since the early 1990s, statistics for alcohol-related deaths in the UK in 2007 indicated a levelling-off of the trend (Figure 6.3). There were 8724 alcohol-related deaths in 2007, fewer than in 2006, although this was more than double the 4144 recorded in 1991. The alcohol-related death rate was 13.3 per 100 000 people in 2007, compared with 6.9 per 100 000 in 1991.

Figure 6.3
Alcohol-related deaths in the UK, 1991–2007

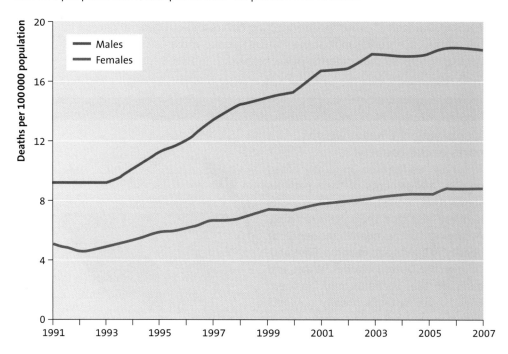

There are more alcohol-related deaths in men than in women (Figure 6.3) – in 2007 the rates were 18.1 deaths per 100 000 and 8.7 per 100 000 respectively. The rate of male deaths had almost doubled from 9.1 per 100 000 in 1991, while female rates had risen from 5.0 per 100 000. In 2007, males accounted for approximately two-thirds of the 8724 deaths.

The trends differ according to age. For males, alcohol-related deaths in those aged 15–34 showed little change (Figure 6.4). Those in the 35–54 age range appeared to level off after 2001, while those in the 75+ category showed a slight decrease. Since 1991, by far the highest alcohol-related death rates have occurred in men aged 55–74: the rate for this group in 2007 was 44.3 per 100 000.

Maps showing the distribution of alcohol-related deaths in the 1990s indicated that central Scotland and the Highlands were particular hotspots. It seems likely that since then England has done some catching up, in that today alcohol abuse has become a leisure pursuit among the wealthier and younger sectors of UK society.

It is premature to think that alcohol-related deaths in the UK have passed their peak. It will only be a matter of time before the current fashion of binge-drinking among

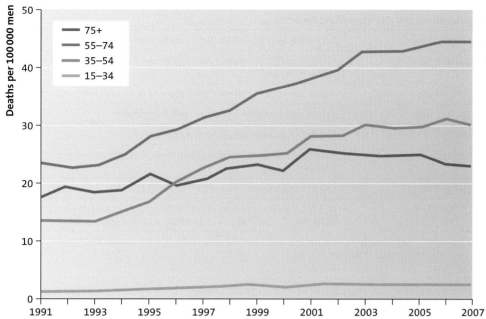

Figure 6.4
*Age-standardised
alcohol death rates
for men, 1991–2007*

teenagers and young adults begins to take its toll on health. Premature deaths will surely follow, most likely among people in their 40s and 50s, as binge-drinking easily leads to alcohol addiction and ultimately to liver failure. It is liver failure that ultimately kills.

Adding to the bad news is the reduction in the productivity of labour, as addicts take time off work because of sickness or hangovers. Think too of the costs to the economy of providing benefits when addicts are no longer capable of working and supporting their dependants, and the cost to the NHS of providing healthcare (*Case study 5*).

Alcohol abuse, like smoking (Case study 45), has considerable health risks as well as economic and social repercussions. The challenge with both is how to break these lifestyle habits.

SMOKING TO AN EARLY DEATH

Case study 45

Lung cancer and more besides

Successive UK governments have done much to discourage smoking. Disincentives include:

- a high tax on tobacco
- health warnings on all tobacco and cigarette packages
- a ban on smoking in all enclosed public places and workplaces
- a ban on tobacco-related advertising
- publicising the proven links between smoking and cancer

Smoking now accounts for one in four cancer deaths in the UK. It is the cause of nine out of ten cases of lung cancer. Tobacco smoke contains at least 80 different

Table 6.2
A positive approach
to anti-smoking

The sooner you give up smoking the better	
After 20 minutes	Your blood pressure and pulse return to normal
After 8 hours	Nicotine, carbon monoxide and oxygen levels in your blood begin to return to normal
After 2 days	Your lungs start to clear and your sense of taste and smell begin to return
After 3 days	Breathing is easier and your energy levels increase
After 2–12 weeks	Circulation improves and exercise gets easier
After 3–9 months	Breathing problems, coughing, shortness of breath and wheezing improve
After 5 years	Risk of having a heart attack falls to about half that of a smoker
After 10 years	Risk of lung cancer falls to about half that of a smoker; you have the same risk of a heart attack as someone who has never smoked

Smoking is very expensive. At today's prices, smoking around 20 cigarettes a day for the next 20 years would cost you over £30 000 in the UK.

cancer-causing substances. When you inhale smoke, these chemicals enter your lungs and spread round the rest of your body. Of all the cancers, lung cancer has one of the lowest survival rates. Smoking also increases the risk of over a dozen other cancers, including cancer of the mouth, larynx, liver, pancreas, kidney, bladder and cervix, as well as some types of leukaemia. Smoking is also a key factor in the incidence of cardiovascular diseases (*Case study 16*).

Smoking kills five times more people than road accidents, HIV/AIDS, murder, suicide or overdoses. Given these high health risks, it is truly amazing that there are so many smokers in the UK. Why? It cannot be out of ignorance, for the risks are widely publicised at school and in the outside world. Sadly, among some of today's young people it is still deemed to be 'cool' to smoke — the threat of premature death can seem a long way off when you are in your teens. Nicotine is a drug, and many people quickly become addicts after their first few cigarettes.

Apart from anti-smoking clinics, nicotine patches and early education about the health risks, what else can be done to reduce the incidence of smoking in the UK? Some have suggested that when it comes to receiving medical treatment on the NHS, smokers should either be given a low priority or made to pay a premium. Perhaps rather than stressing the negatives of smoking, the focus should be on the positives of giving up (Table 6.2).

Despite all the health risk warnings, smoking continues to be the prime lifestyle killer in the UK. What can be done to reduce this lifestyle habit?

Uncertain causes

There are some prevalent non-infectious diseases in the UK, the causes of which remain uncertain. Are they linked to lifestyles or genetics? Breast cancer is one such disease.

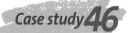

BREAST CANCER IN THE UK

A cause for concern?

Breast cancer is now the most common cancer in the UK. More than 45 000 women a year are diagnosed with breast cancer, and incidence rates have increased by more than 50% over the last 25 years. In 2007, breast cancer accounted for 8% of all cancer deaths (bearing in mind that it is very rare among men).

The reasons for the steady rise in breast cancer in the UK over the last 30 years are unclear. Certainly, mass screening programmes, which started in 1988, have played a part in raising the number of diagnosed cases. They are responsible for the diagnosis of a quarter of new cases (Figure 6.5). It is reckoned that the NHS programme in England saves around 1400 lives each year. Improvements in awareness of the symptoms of the disease and better health education are also helping to increase detection. Breast cancer is age-related, and since women are living longer than in the past it is hardly surprising that its incidence is on the rise. Eight out of ten breast cancers are diagnosed in women aged 50 and over. But a number of lifestyle factors may also be contributing to the upward trend. For example, more women are choosing to have children later in life, and this is now thought to increase the chances of developing the disease. Obesity in post-menopausal women is thought to be a risk factor. As with most forms of cancer, the genetic factor is important, but perhaps there are others of which we are as yet unaware. There could be a link with environmental pollution or with food. Who knows?

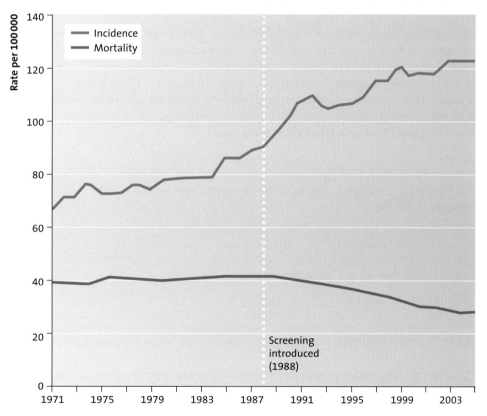

Figure 6.5
Female breast cancer in the UK — incidence and mortality, 1971–2005

Earlier detection and improved treatment have meant that survival rates have risen and mortality rates have fallen (Figure 6.5). Currently, the mortality rate in England is 28 deaths per 100 000 women. It is the second most common cause of cancer death in women, after lung cancer.

This case study illustrates the important point that for all our modern medical research there are still common diseases, the causes of which remain unconfirmed.

33

Using case studies

Question

Describe and explain the concerns associated with the continuing rise in breast cancer in the UK.

Guidance

Work under the headings of: causes, treatment, costs.
Visit **www.cancerresearchuk.org/breast cancer**
   www.breastcancer.org.uk/

Morbidity factors

In explaining spatial variations in the incidence of health problems and diseases (for example, in Figure 6.2), a number of factors need to be taken into account. These include:

■ demographic — spatial variations in the age structure of the population
■ economic — spatial variations in unemployment and the general level of affluence
■ social — spatial variations in the mix of social classes
■ healthcare — spatial variations in its quality

34

Using case studies

Question

With reference to Figure 6.2 (*Case study 43*), describe and try to explain the spatial distribution of obesity in the UK.

Guidance

Your description should focus on the most obvious features of the distribution pattern. In seeking a possible explanation, work through the main factor categories given above.

When it comes to the last factor, treatment and the quality of healthcare, it often depends on where you happen to live. Despite the fact that the NHS (*Case study 49*) strives to achieve uniformity in the quality of healthcare across the country, the way healthcare is delivered, by means of primary care trusts, results in considerable variations from place to place. These variations give rise to what are known as health's 'postcode lotteries' (*Case study 47*).

POSTCODE LOTTERIES

A revealing analysis

The NHS spends far more on treating people with diseases such as cancer and heart disease in some areas of the UK than in others, a study has found. The King's Fund, which carried out the analysis, says that after adjustment for the age and health of the population, there is little explanation for the striking variation in spending from one primary care trust (PCT) to another, and it probably cannot always be justified. The research suggests that a postcode lottery in care exists around the country that is not just about the well-publicised reluctance of some PCTs to fund certain new and expensive drugs.

The National Institute for Health and Clinical Excellence (NICE) was set up to put a stop to the medicines lottery. All drugs recommended by NICE have to be funded by every PCT in England and Wales, with similar arrangements for Scotland. But the King's Fund survey suggests that the amount spent per patient with cancer, mental illness or circulatory diseases such as heart disease varies greatly from one PCT to another.

Middlesbrough PCT, for example, spends £167 per head on circulatory diseases such as heart disease, but Southwark (London) spends £76. Knowsley PCT spends an average of £118 on a man with cancer, while Ealing (London) spends £47. Islington (London) spends £332 per head of its population on mental health, the East Riding of Yorkshire £114. Factors underlying these variations include differences in the efficiency of hospitals and the decisions of individual doctors about whom and when to treat, and what sort of treatment to provide. But the findings also raise questions about the consistency of the decisions PCTs make about how much they spend on different diseases.

The King Fund's chief executive has said:

> The survey raised more questions than answers. It does not mean that any one PCT's spending is necessarily wrong, but it does suggest that as well as unexplained variations in clinical practice, there are unexplained spending variations. Some of these are almost certainly not justified. We need better information about what PCTs spend their money on and what gains in health they achieve.

But should people's decisions about where to live be determined by their particular medical conditions and the allocation of resources by particular PCTs?

This case study raises a number of questions. Is this information about the relative performance and expenditures of PCTs readily available in the public domain and in an easily comprehensible form? Should people be given the option of seeking medical treatment outside their PCT, or should they be required to move?

35

As a class, discuss the last question posed in the concluding summary of *Case study 47*.

Guidance

The question raises broader issues of social justice and freedom of choice. Where do you stand on these issues?

Using case studies

Verdict

So far, this UK health check has been a mix of good and bad results. The good news concerns notable successes in reducing the incidence of infectious diseases. Some have been virtually eliminated. However, the bad news concerns the rising morbidity and mortality of non-infectious diseases, particularly those that are associated with affluence and lifestyles. So what is the overall verdict — does the good news outweigh the bad? Perhaps the best summing-up is provided in trends in life expectancies.

Case study 48 RECENT CHANGES IN UK LIFE EXPECTANCY

Is it all good news?

The four maps that make up Figure 6.6 tell us two things:

- Life expectancy continues to be significantly higher for women.
- Impressive improvements in life expectancy during the period 1992–2006 have been sustained by both males and females.

Over the 14 years illustrated by the maps, life expectancy consistently increased, rising from 73.4 years to 77.3 years for men and from 78.9 years to 81.5 years for women. The largest increases over this period for both sexes occurred in England and Wales. The smallest increase was in Scotland for males and in Northern Ireland for females.

The map for men is the clearer in showing the way longevity has crept up the country. However, there are still parts of the UK where life expectancy is well below that for the rest of western Europe. Glasgow and the Outer Hebrides are two such examples. For women, it is broadly the same story, with increasing life expectancy 'moving' northwards — although there are pockets in all regions where progress is slower.

In 2006 the local area with the highest life expectancy for both males (83.7 years) and females (87.8 years) was Kensington and Chelsea. In contrast, the local area with the lowest life expectancy was Glasgow (70.8 years for males and 77.1 years for females). One possible conclusion to be drawn from these maps is that for every hour you live, your life expectancy increases by 16 minutes.

On the face of it, Figure 6.6 is the bearer of good news. The 2006 maps certainly reflect improvements in medical research and healthcare, both of which have the potential to extend life. But while the medical profession has waged a fairly successful battle against many infectious diseases (with the notable exception of HIV/AIDS), there are aspects of our modern lifestyles that carry potentially severe health risks. It will be interesting to see the pattern of life expectancy changes in, say, 25 years' time. Will our obsessions with food, drink and drugs and their related deaths turn the tide of rising life expectancy?

Another worrying fact has emerged in a recent report on health inequalities. It is that people living in the country's poorest areas live an average of 7 years less than those in the richest ones.

Finally, one vital question — which is more important: length of life or quality of life? Can we be sure that in extending life expectancy, we are extending the number of

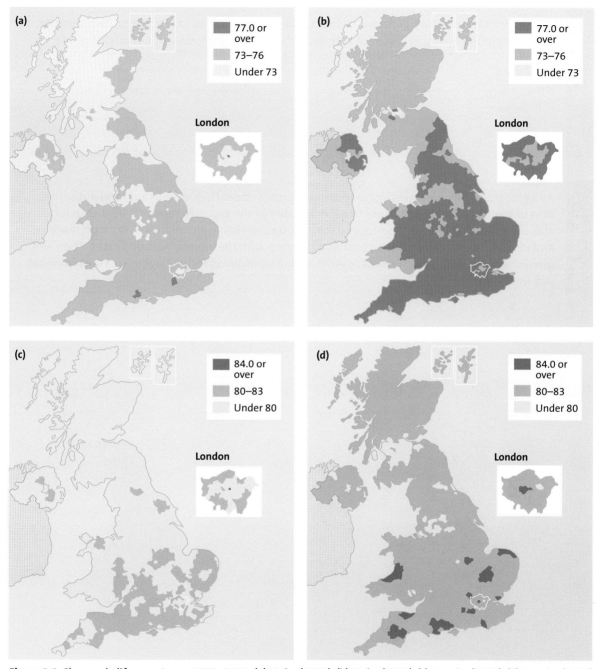

Figure 6.6 *Changes in life expectancy, 1992–2006: (a) Males (1992), (b) Males (2006), (c) Females (1992), (d) Females (2006)*

'quality' years? That clearly is a challenge to society as a whole and to healthcare in particular.

Besides the last question, two others raised by this case study relate to the issue of equality. Should we be concerned about these spatial variations in life expectancy? Is there any chance of reducing them?

36

Using case studies

Divide your class into two groups and debate the question raised at the end of *Case study 48*, with one group arguing in favour of length of life and the other in favour of quality of life.

Guidance

Think outside the frame of just the individual. Consider the economic and social implications of both options.

37

Using case studies

As a group, identify and investigate ten major causes of death in either your local authority area or the UK. Allocate one cause to each member of the group to research. Visit your local authority website: relevant mortality data are often available at ward level. Print off maps and identify the area with the highest and the area with the lowest mortality rates. Then as a group compare your maps. To what extent do the same areas recur? Suggest reasons for what you find.

Healthcare provision

Healthcare is something of an umbrella term covering a range of goods and services aimed at promoting good health and dealing with disease. The promotion of good health relies heavily on education (about hygiene, sensible lifestyles and health risks) and access to services: medical, dental and pharmaceutical. Dealing with disease involves three main types of action:

- **preventive** — for example, immunisation, vaccination and screening programmes
- **curative** — for example, a course of drugs or a surgical operation
- **palliative** — for example, nursing people with terminal illnesses

In countries with well established healthcare systems, three levels of provision are widely recognised:

- Primary healthcare is provided in the home or at a clinic or health centre. Such care commonly includes basic medical attention from a GP or a nurse attached to a health centre. The services offered include diagnosing illnesses, prescribing medication, immunising children and screening for some diseases. The services are offered locally, since they will be accessed quite frequently.
- Secondary healthcare is essentially that offered in hospitals, where patients are admitted for treatment that cannot take place in a clinic or health centre. Patients are usually referred to a hospital by their local GP for diagnosis, further investigation and treatment (including surgery). The secondary sector is therefore more specialised and will often be less concerned with prevention and more with cure.

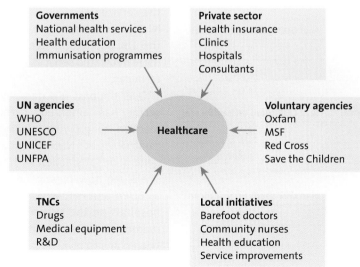

Governments
National health services
Health education
Immunisation programmes

Private sector
Health insurance
Clinics
Hospitals
Consultants

UN agencies
WHO
UNESCO
UNICEF
UNFPA

Healthcare

Voluntary agencies
Oxfam
MSF
Red Cross
Save the Children

TNCs
Drugs
Medical equipment
R&D

Local initiatives
Barefoot doctors
Community nurses
Health education
Service improvements

Figure 7.1
Healthcare providers

- Tertiary healthcare is about the delivery of even more specialist investigation and treatment. Typical here are hospitals that specialise in the diagnosis and treatment of cancer, or undertake heart and transplant surgery.

Figure 7.1 shows the main providers of healthcare.

Government provision

In most HICs, people look to their government to deliver healthcare through some form of national or state-run scheme, such as the NHS in the UK. Such schemes are usually funded by revenues that governments collect either indirectly through income tax or directly through some form of national insurance. The idea is that all working people contribute and as a consequence there is 'free' access to healthcare goods and services for all contributors and their dependants (*Case study 49*).

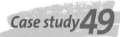 **Case study 49** | **THE UK'S NATIONAL HEALTH SERVICE (NHS)**

Healthcare under pressure

The NHS was set up in 1948 to provide healthcare on the basis of need rather than ability to pay. It was a landmark achievement of the post-war Labour government. The NHS is funded by general taxation and taxes levied on those in employment (National Insurance). Access to healthcare is usually by registration with a general practitioner (GP), who is responsible when appropriate for referring patients to secondary healthcare. The NHS is administered by Health Authorities — now referred to as 'trusts'. These are given budgets by the government to spend on hospital and community health services. They are also responsible for monitoring the health and the care needs of the populations within their areas. General practices are organised into primary care trusts.

The target of much criticism in recent years, the NHS has undergone a raft of reforms aimed at improving the service. Despite this, it has remained a burning party political issue, with debates about whether putting increasing amounts of public money into the service will solve its problems. The NHS is under pressure, particularly as the UK population ages and requires more dedicated services and more long-term care.

Over the past few decades, a private sector has emerged, perhaps as a reaction to growing waiting lists for treatment at NHS hospitals and a general dissatisfaction with the service. There are now private providers, such as BUPA and PPP, which run their own hospitals on the subscriptions paid by members. More recently, there have been plans to involve the private sector in running the NHS. In short, the UK

Table 7.1
Percentage of GDP spent on public healthcare in selected countries

Country (HICs)	% of GDP spent on healthcare
Japan	8.1
UK	9.4
USA	16.0
Country (MICs)	**% of GDP spent on healthcare**
Brazil	8.0
China	4.8
India	5.0
Country (LICs)	**% of GDP spent on healthcare**
Ethiopia	4.1
Nepal	5.3
Ecuador	3.5

seems to be moving gently towards of mode of healthcare more akin to that which has prevailed in the USA (*Case study 51*).

The UK can be rightly proud of the NHS. It has served the country well for over 60 years. It does, however, have its current shortcomings.

Providing a national health service requires huge sums of money, particularly given the sophisticated technology involved in today's healthcare (scanners, micro-surgery, radiotherapy, etc.), and the ageing populations of most HICs enhance the demand for healthcare. Inevitably, healthcare can consume a significant slice of a country's GDP (Table 7.1). Not only that, but the question of how much or how little should be spent on healthcare is often a hotly debated political issue.

State health schemes are very much a feature of socialist and communist countries. Although the number of such countries is now much lower than it was two decades ago, Cuba's healthcare system continues to be the focus of much foreign interest and indeed admiration (*Case study 50*).

HEALTHCARE IN CUBA

Case study **50**

An impressive model

An uprising in the Caribbean island state of Cuba led to the establishment of a communist regime that prevails to this day. One of the country's most widely acclaimed achievements has been its healthcare system, which is free to every citizen by right. Basic health indicators are head and shoulders above the norms for less developed countries — and in some cases are ahead of those for developed countries. Its achievements are even more remarkable bearing in mind that Cuba has a per capita GDP figure lower than that of many other Latin American countries, and less than around one-fiftieth of the USA's. The achievements are also remarkable in that for much of the time, Cuba has been 'isolated' from the global community, largely as a result a US-led embargo on foreign trade.

There is a tiered system of healthcare delivery in Cuba, from (1) the *consultorios* (small three-storey buildings where the ground floor is the clinic, the first floor is a doctor's flat and the third floor a nurse's flat) to (2) polyclinics; from (3) hospitals to (4) national medical research institutions. Medical services are available from one end of this elongated island to the other. There are 30 000 GPs, roughly the same number as in the UK, but Cuba has only one-fifth of the population. Cuba has 21 medical schools, while the UK has only 12.

Life expectancy for men and women in Cuba today is exactly the same as in the UK. However, there is one major difference between Cuba's health statistics and those of the UK. In the UK healthcare costs around $2723 per person annually; in Cuba it costs a mere $310.

Such is the standard of healthcare in Cuba that the country is now making its services available to other countries as a 'commodity' in international trade. As noted earlier (*Case study 40*), Cuba and Venezuela have an agreement whereby medical services, in particular surgery, are traded for crude oil.

Cuba's healthcare service stands as an example for the world to follow. It is efficient, relatively cheap and socially equitable.

The private sector

Despite the delivery of healthcare by governments, there are often parallel services being run in a private sector. These are supported by those people who are able take out expensive medical insurance to meet the costs of a fast track to good-quality services. Many of them have been 'driven' into the private sector by long waiting lists for operations and some concern about the quality of treatment in the public sector. In some developed countries, most notably the USA, there is a heavy reliance on the private healthcare sector. This is fine for those with a regular income that meets the costs of monthly or annual contributions to a private health scheme. But what do people living at or near the poverty line do?

Case study 51 — HEALTHCARE IN THE USA

A divided nation

One of the election promises made by President Obama in 2009 was to reform the US healthcare system. The USA currently spends 16% of its GDP on healthcare. This compares with a figure of 9.4% for the UK. The USA has several types of privately and publicly funded health insurance plans that provide healthcare services:

- Over half of the population is currently covered by employment-based health insurance, either directly or through a trade union, with continued benefits available to retired workers.
- Around a quarter are covered by government-funded programmes such as Medicaid (for low-income earners), Medicare (for people over 65 and those with disabilities) and the State Children's Health Insurance Program (SCHIP), which provides for children whose family income is too high to qualify for Medicaid. These schemes are funded by state and federal taxes.
- Self-employed people generally purchase their own health insurance.

It is estimated that 15% of the population has no medical insurance whatsoever. They are often among the poorest people in the USA, but medical treatment, even for the most basic conditions, is very expensive. Today a growing number of employers offer no health benefits to their employees or have reduced benefits. Benefits have been withdrawn from retirees. Because of the growing expense, states that once had generous government-funded healthcare policies are cutting back, and in some cases capping the number of people served by a programme.

President Obama has expressed his commitment to controlling rising healthcare costs, guaranteeing choice of doctor, and assuring high-quality, affordable healthcare for all Americans. Rapidly escalating health costs are crushing family, business and government budgets. Employer-sponsored health insurance premiums have doubled in the last 9 years, a rate three times faster than cumulative wage increases. This forces some families to sit around the kitchen table to make impossible choices between paying either rent or health premiums.

The US government believes there is a need for a comprehensive overhaul of the healthcare system. The reforms should:

- reduce long-term growth of healthcare costs for businesses and government
- protect families from bankruptcy or debt because of healthcare costs

Figure 7.2
Protests in Pennsylvania about health reforms in the USA, August 2009

- guarantee choice of doctors and health plans
- invest in prevention and wellness
- improve patient safety and quality of care
- assure affordable, quality health coverage for all Americans
- maintain coverage when people change or lose their job
- remove barriers to healthcare coverage for people with pre-existing medical conditions

To anyone living outside the USA, the resistance within that country to President Obama's healthcare campaign might seem incredible. But surveys have shown an across-the-board uncertainty about how or whether the healthcare overhaul would affect individuals or the country as a whole. There has also been concern about how changes and restrictions needed to pay for the overhaul would affect household budgets. In one national poll, only 27% thought that they would be better off personally as a result of the reforms, with 30% suspecting they would be worse off, and 36% predicting not much difference.

In the meantime, thousands of people have been suffering or dying prematurely because they cannot afford to pay for medical treatment. Truly, a case of health risk!

The challenge for the USA is to provide public healthcare in a country driven by private enterprise and by the perception that provision by government is tantamount to communism.

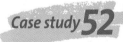
Question

What are the arguments in favour of a national health service?

Guidance

The arguments are to be found in issues of access and social justice.

Two more international providers

In Part 5 the point was made that one of the outcomes of economic globalisation was the emergence of significant players in the delivery of healthcare and as guardians of global health, namely the international aid organisations (*Case study 37*) and the pharmaceutical TNCs (*Case study 35*). The next case studies look at two more important international providers, namely the WHO and one representative of a large number of voluntary international agencies.

Case study 52 | THE WORLD HEALTH ORGANIZATION (WHO)

Guardians and promoters of global health

The WHO was set up in 1948 by the United Nations (UN). It is one of some ten UN agencies broadly concerned with welfare; others include the Food and Agriculture Organization (FAO), the United Nations International Children's Emergency Fund (UNICEF) and the United Nations Relief and Works Agency (UNRWA). No fewer than 193 states are members of the WHO. Currently, its main objectives are:

- promoting development — encouraging investment in healthcare and the principle of equal access
- fostering health security — by being constantly on the lookout for outbreaks of emerging and epidemic-prone diseases
- strengthening health systems — ensuring that health services reach the poor
- harnessing research, information and evidence — monitoring the global health situation
- enhancing partnerships — between the WHO and other international organisations, donors and the private sector

Among the successes of the WHO have been the eradication of smallpox and polio, but much still needs to be done in terms of expanding primary healthcare to the poorer parts and poorer communities of the world.

xzoex/Fotolia

***Figure 7.3** Emblem of the World Health Organization*

The WHO has effectively been the guardian of the world's health. Its success has been due in no small measure to the support it receives from the individual countries of the world.

MÉDECINS SANS FRONTIÈRES (MSF)

Provider of emergency medical help

MSF is an international and independent humanitarian organisation principally concerned with delivering medical help during emergencies such as epidemics, natural disasters and armed conflicts. It was set up in 1971 by a group of French doctors. It has since grown into an organisation of international proportions with offices in 18 countries and ongoing projects in over 70 countries. There are more than 2500 volunteer medics working worldwide and alongside thousands of local personnel.

MSF's main activities include:

■ helping with vaccination programmes, particularly during epidemics
■ providing help with clean water and proper sanitation
■ refurbishing hospitals, clinics and dispensaries, particularly those damaged by war or natural disasters
■ working in very remote rural areas and urban slums
■ training local personnel in healthcare matters

Its medical activities in 2009 included:

■ providing medical and social care to homeless people living in Romania's capital city, Bucharest
■ providing free healthcare to something like 2 million Afghan refugees in Iran
■ treating HIV/AIDS patients in Laos with anti-retroviral therapy (ART)
■ dealing with the physical and psychological injuries suffered by Palestinians as a result of the Israeli bombardment of Gaza
■ helping to meet the medical needs of Haiti following a succession of natural disasters (Figure 7.4)

Bob Edme/AP/Press Association Images

Figure 7.4 *Members of the French NGO Médecins Sans Frontières (Doctors Without Borders) oversee the loading of a plane with aid bound for earthquake-hit Haiti, in January 2010*

MSF is not the only non-governmental organisation providing emergency aid. Others include Oxfam, Christian Aid, CAFOD and Save the Children, but it is distinguished by its focus on medical assistance.

39 Question

What do you think are the advantages that non-governmental organisations have over governmental organisations when it comes to providing health aid?

Guidance

Think about those political situations that generate a need for emergency health aid.

Using case studies

Local initiatives

An important point to make here is that grassroots initiatives in poorer and less developed countries can offer a crucial way of overcoming two obstacles to adequate healthcare provision: a lack of public money because of low GDP, and a shortage of trained medical staff.

The term **barefoot doctor** was first used to describe a system of healthcare established in China under the Communist regime of Chairman Mao Zedong. Men and women were selected to receive a limited amount of formal training as health educators. This meant that they could provide basic medical services at a local level, such as advising on how to cope with common diseases and helping to educate local communities in preventive healthcare matters such as diet, hygiene and family planning. The system proved a huge success in China and has since been widely imitated in many developing countries, where its use is now quite widespread.

Over the past three decades, government-run health services in developing countries have begun to tap into the rich reservoir of skills found among traditional healers and traditional birth attendants, to help offset the shortage of trained doctors and nurses. China has up to 20 times more homoeopathic doctors than it has conventionally trained medics. In Africa, there is one traditional healer for every 5000 people, compared with one doctor for every 28 000 people.

The mobile phone is fast becoming a basic part of global everyday life. There are already local initiatives capitalising on the healthcare opportunities that mobiles can provide. In the UK, for example, some health authorities are putting the mobile to good use (*Case study 54*).

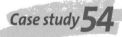 *Case study* 54   MOBILE PHONES AND HEALTHCARE IN THE UK

Making the most of modern communications

The frequent use of mobile phones has been in the news in recent years as a possible health risk. But mobiles are now being put to good medical use and reducing health risks. It looks as if they can help improve the lives of thousands of Britons who suffer from chronic diseases such as diabetes and asthma.

Eight primary care trusts are now using software that can be downloaded onto ordinary mobile phones. Initial trials involving people suffering from diabetes have shown that the software, costing about £250, can significantly reduce the complications associated with chronic disorders and prevent hospital admissions.

The software enables patients to record details of their condition and its treatment. This means that they can better monitor and manage their condition between visits to their doctor or specialist. The data collected are also sent automatically to a central monitoring service, which alerts nurses to potentially dangerous changes in a patient's condition. Those at risk can then be seen immediately by a specialist. As a result of the monitoring, there is a significant reduction in the risk of complications, such as blindness and the need for amputations, associated with diabetes.

Contemporary Case Studies

Another version of the program can monitor the side-effects of chemotherapy, so that the oncologist can adjust doses if necessary. Other systems are being made available for asthma, high blood pressure and chronic obstructive pulmonary disease (COPD), a lung condition often linked to smoking.

The mobile phone is now an established utensil of everyday life. Rates of ownership are rising in all parts of the world. This case study illustrates its potential value in the context of healthcare.

It would be wrong to think that the health-care opportunities offered by the mobile phone are confined to the developed world. Mobile phone networks and owner-ship are also expanding in less developed parts of the world. The extension of server networks is easier and cheaper than creat-ing new landline networks.

Figure 7.5
Mobile phones can now reduce health risks

Andres Rodriguez/Fotolia

BRINGING HEALTHCARE TO REMOTE INDIA

Case study **55**

The Teledoc project

Providing healthcare to remote rural areas is a challenge for most countries, particularly for a large and emerging economy such as India. It is estimated that India has around 700 000 villages. Nearly half of them have populations of under 500 people, and about a quarter of them have no doctor. Adding to the problem is the true remoteness of many of these villages. They are only accessible by long and often hazardous tracks.

An organisation called Jiva has recently come up with one solution to this challenge. It lies in taking advantage of modern communications technology in the form of a GPRS-enabled Java application. Each of the 30 remote villages chosen to participate in the initial trial has a Teledoc or field representative. These villagers note a patient's symptoms and then use mobile phones to transmit the information over the internet to a central database. The mobiles also have cameras so that images of injuries and infections can be sent, helping to make for a more accurate diagnosis of the medical condition. After analysis of the information, the Teledoc is advised as to what best to do for the patient.

Preliminary results from the trial show that some 30 000 people have benefited from the Jiva project. Efforts are now being made to expand this e-healthcare. It will need the help of a major corporation to roll out the project across the country. At the time of writing, discussions are taking place with ITC Ltd, one of India's biggest companies.

The Teledoc project is a prime example of how the mobile phone might be put to good use in terms of bringing much-needed healthcare to remote parts of India.

Access to healthcare

Having examined the providers of healthcare, we should now look at the other side of the coin — the recipients. Access to healthcare is largely conditioned by:

■ where you live on the planet
■ where you are on the affluence scale

If you live in an HIC, close to the capital city, and are reasonably well off, you can expect to access the best possible healthcare, particularly if you are able and willing to pay. On the other hand, if you are poor and live in a remote part of an LIC, perhaps the best you can expect is to access some very basic primary healthcare, possibly provided by an aid charity. Between these two extremes there is a host of intermediate circumstances. The inequality of access is well illustrated by the percentages of national populations with regular access to essential drugs (Figure 7.6).

Looking at the global situation, there is a huge mismatch between the need for healthcare and the level of provision. The mismatch is most acute at the 'least developed' end of the development scale. This point is illustrated by Figure 7.7. Figure 7.7(a) shows the level of need by global region. The measure used here is the burden of disease. Well over half the global burden is borne by China, India and sub-Saharan Africa. However, when it comes to provision of healthcare, as shown by Figure 7.7(b), well over 75% of the global provision is made in the established market economies, i.e. in the HICs and some MICs.

At a global scale, access to healthcare is inversely proportional to the level of poverty. That same relationship also applies even within the more affluent countries. Poor urban areas, for example, are generally characterised by inferior healthcare. But spatial unevenness in the quality of healthcare is also caused by other factors. In the UK, there are differences in the priorities and spending of individual primary

Figure 7.6
Regular access to essential drugs (percentage of population)

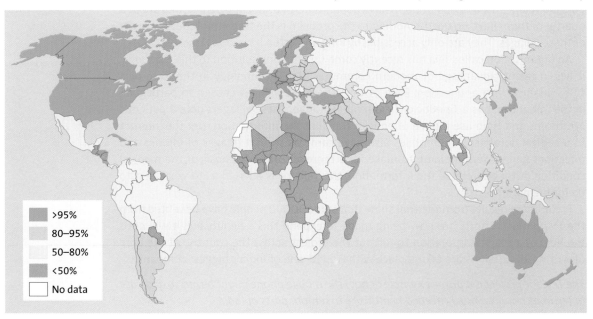

>95%
80–95%
50–80%
<50%
No data

(a) The global burden of disease
(% of disability life years)

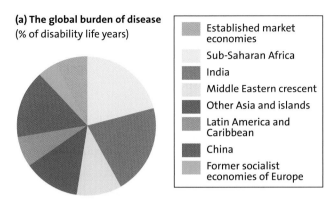

Established market economies

Sub-Saharan Africa

India

Middle Eastern crescent

Other Asia and islands

Latin America and Caribbean

China

Former socialist economies of Europe

(b) Global health expenditure
(% of health expenditure worldwide)

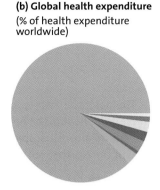

Figure 7.7
The global healthcare disparity

care trusts, which deliver the NHS at the grassroots level. These differences give rise to what is now widely referred to as the health's postcode lottery (*Case study 47*). Where you live can have an important bearing (*Case study 56*).

WHO YOU ARE AND WHERE YOU LIVE

Case study **56**

Factors affecting morbidity and mortality

The basic message of many of the preceding case studies is that both morbidity and disease-related mortality vary from place to place across the globe. What are the factors underlying these spatial variations? To put that question in a personal form: why is it that you will contract some diseases and not other, and why is it that you will die of a particular disease and not others? Figure 7.8 identifies some of the more significant

Figure 7.8
Where you live — life or death?

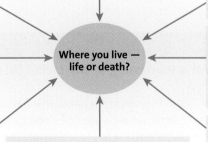

Water
Safety of water is paramount. Soft water has been linked with high rates of heart disease. Trace elements in water, such as nickel, cadmium, mercury and lead, are also hazardous in excess. High concentrations of aluminium in water have been linked with variations in Alzheimer's

Genetics
There is strong evidence that people with blood group A have greater immunity to disease than those with blood group O. There may be other genetic factors that make some populations more susceptible to certain diseases.

Housing
Size of dwelling is not important compared with its quality of weather-proofness, safety, ventilation and services (water supply and sewage). The risk of accidental death is high in unsafe dwellings. Security from natural hazards (flooding, fog etc.) and human hazards (noise, traffic etc.).

Climate
Health studies have linked cold winters and high rainfall with high death rates from heart disease, strokes and pneumonia. Overcast skies and damp conditions correlate with increased rates of depression.

Where you live — life or death?

Lifestyle
Poor diet and excessive drinking are thought to impact less on variations in health than smoking. But all three significantly increase the risk of heart disease and cancer.

Pollution
Although air pollution created by the burning of coal has been greatly reduced, another cause has taken its place. Petrochemical pollution caused by motor vehicle exhausts may be partly responsible for the higher death rates from respiratory illness in major cities and allergic reactions such as asthma attacks.

Radiation
Background radiation varies from place to place and may play a part in some diseases. Doses of radiation that are above the limit deemed to be acceptable in the nuclear industry are emitted as radon by granite rocks. Radon is claimed to account for 1 in 20 cases of lung cancer in the UK.

Access to services
If you fall ill, the treatment you receive depends on the quality of the medical services available in the area where you live. Even in those countries where there is a national health service, the matching of services to need varies spatially. Richer areas and richer sections of the population usually enjoy the best health services.

factors. They may be broadly grouped into (1) those related to who you are and (2) those related to where you live.

First, there are the three aspects of 'who you are' — your genes, your socioeconomic class and your lifestyle. Researchers continue to discover the immense significance of our genes and DNA, particularly in explaining why we succumb to specific non-infectious diseases.

The postcode lottery idea (*Case study 47*) may be extended to embrace the whole globe. Your health, the health risks you face and the quality of healthcare you receive all depend to a considerable extent on where you live in the world, particularly on which side of the North–South divide you happen to be born.

The world is rich in inequalities. Access to healthcare is a prime example.

40

Using case studies

Question

Illustrate and explain the links between the three aspects of 'who you are' and disease.

Guidance

The distinction between infectious and non-infectious diseases will be vital to your answer. Affluence and poverty should figure in your response.

Preparing for pandemics

Finally, we look at healthcare from a slightly different viewpoint, namely in its rather more defensive role of containing specific diseases. Given the movement of people around the world in these days of economic globalisation, it is hardly surprising that pandemics are increasing in frequency and spatial extent. *Case study 57* looks at the contingency plans that governments and major international players drew up to cope with the anticipated worsening of the swine flu pandemic.

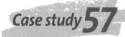

Case study **57** SWINE FLU

Preparing for a worsening of the swine flu pandemic — the world takes guard

By the end of 2009, the swine flu pandemic had claimed a relatively small number of deaths. However, international agencies and governments and healthcare authorities across the globe were putting in place a whole range of precautionary measures just in case the H1N1 virus turned nasty and became a serious killer (*Case study 38*).

The following is a selection of actions at two different spatial scales from around the world.

Global

■ The WHO estimated that worldwide production of the vaccine needed to be at least 3 billion doses per year. It warned that in some areas the demand for vaccination was already greater than the supply, but the gap was narrowing. It recommended that health workers be given first priority for early vaccination to protect themselves and their patients, and thus help keep healthcare systems functioning as the pandemic evolved. It also urged that those groups most at risk should be identified and given priority for vaccination.

■ The World Bank set aside funds to help countries meet the costs of checking the spread of the virus. Mexico was the first recipient.

National

■ UK — People who had swine flu symptoms were given a unique access number and told where their nearest antiviral collection point was. They were then recommended to ask a friend or relative who did not have swine flu to pick up their antivirals from the nearest collection point. The flu friend would have to show their own identification details as well as those of the patient. A dedicated website was set up to provide information about all aspects of the disease. A nationwide vaccination programme was also ready to roll.

Figure 7.9
UK swine flu poster (Department of Health 2009)

Crown copyright (Click-Use PSI licence number C2007001851)

■ USA — President Obama declared a state of emergency. The emergency rules effectively cut through official red tape and freed up resources to respond much faster in the event of a serious outbreak. They also made it much easier for hospitals to quickly treat and process any large and sudde n influx of patients infected with swine flu, the H1N1 virus. Military personnel were to be given priority for vaccination.

■ India — Schools and colleges in areas where outbreaks occurred were closed for at least a week. The government installed compulsory health screening facilities for passengers from flu-affected countries at 22 international airports. A government official said that India had plenty of Tamiflu, the drug used to treat swine flu, but it had not yet been put on open sale.

■ China — International travellers arriving in the country had their temperatures taken. Anyone with an above-normal temperature was put into quarantine and tested for swine flu. China produced its own vaccine and in October 2009 launched a mass vaccination campaign.

■ Ethiopia — A remote sensor to detect flu symptoms in passengers on incoming flights was installed at Addis Ababa international airport. The country did not have any vaccine stocks.

Preparations varied from country to country and were strongly influenced by national levels of development and affluence, as well as by government perceptions of the threat. Even the poorest countries were persuaded to act, albeit minimally.

There is a growing realisation that we need to be much more proactive in the fight against infectious diseases. Rather than drawing up contingency plans and then waiting for outbreaks to happen, we need to do more by way of outright prevention. Appropriate actions would include implementing 'saturation' vaccination programmes and removing causal factors, particularly those of an environmental kind. Such actions would promise both better health and the reduction of health risks.

41

Using case studies

Question

Do you think that the swine flu pandemic has been overpublicised by the media? Are the action plans related to the level of threat (possible mortality rates)? Give your reasons.

Guidance

Think of the criteria used in the definition of a pandemic, and criteria that might be used to assess its seriousness.

Examination advice

The case studies that have been an integral part of your A-level geography course have been included principally to illustrate and help you understand theoretical ideas and particular contemporary issues. The same case studies also serve a third purpose, namely to be put to good use in a variety of ways in the examination. Much depends on:

■ the question task and the command used in the wording of a question. Table 8.1 indicates that there are at least four different question scenarios. They are ranked according to what is expected in terms of the degree of case study detail. They range from a simple name-dropping to a detailed knowledge and understanding of a particular situation, issue or idea.

Table 8.1
Question commands and the examiner's case study and text expectations

Increasing requirement for case study detail →

Task or command*	Name	Support	Compare / contrast	Examine / explain (a particular situation or statement)
Typical question	Name one country in which there is a high rate of maternal mortality	With the use of examples, identify the health risks associated with environmental pollution	Compare the healthcare systems of any two countries	With reference to specific diseases, examine the different ways in which infectious diseases are spread
Case study expectation	No more than the name of an appropriate country, e.g. Ethiopia, Bangladesh	At least two case studies for air pollution and two for water pollution	Better to opt for two contrasting case studies, e.g. UK and USA	One infectious disease for each different means of transmission
Text requirement	One sentence	Two or three sentences per example	Extended prose	In-depth extended prose

*A word of caution — watch out for those questions that do not specifically ask for examples, but nonetheless expect them. For example:
● Suggest reasons why some areas are more prone to disease than others.
● 'Globalisation creates health risks.' Discuss.
● To what extent do you agree that the swine flu threat was exaggerated?
If you are in doubt as to whether examples are required in your answer to a question, it is better to give some than to give none, but not of the 'e.g. Africa' kind!

■ the context of the question — the challenge here is to find an example or case study that is appropriate to the question topic. Table 8.2 may help, as it links the case studies presented in this book to the main topic areas of health and health risks.

Table 8.2 *A matrix relating case studies in this book to the main topics of health and health risks*

Topic	See case study	Topic	See case study
The global dimension		**Infectious disease**	
1 Patterns of health and health risks	1, ,2, 7	1 Diversity	3, 7
2 Pharmaceutical companies	35, 36	2 Conquered diseases	6, 8
3 International aid	37, 52, 53	3 Contained diseases	9
4 Migration and the spread of disease	38, 39	4 Emerging diseases	10
5 Medical tourism	40	5 Re-emerging diseases	11
6 Preparing for pandemics	34, 38, 57	6 Sporadic diseases	9, 12
Non-infectious diseases		7 Unconquered diseases	13, 34
1 Diseases of ageing	14, 15, 31, 42	**Impacts of disease**	
2 Lifestyle diseases	5, 16, 17, 18, 19, 30, 43, 44	1 Demographic	1, 34, 38
3 Diseases linked to pollution	21, 22, 23, 24, 25, 26, 27	2 Social	31, 34, 42, 43, 44
4 Diseases associated with pregnancy, childbirth and infants	4, 27, 29	3 Economic	32, 34, 43, 44
Healthcare	47, 49, 50, 51, 52, 53, 54, 55, 56	4 Environmental	33, 34

In the remaining sections, we look at five different examination contexts that require the use of case studies. Four are shown in Table 8.1: they apply mainly to unseen examination papers. The fifth is where the geography specification requires you to research a set topic and to submit a report by a given deadline. So those contexts range from simply naming a case study as an example of some particular situation, through use of case study material for support purposes, to an extended and detailed use of case studies.

Naming examples

This requires nothing more than being able to cite one of your case studies as a relevant example. The test here is basically one of appropriateness. You need do no more than to name one.

42 Question

Name one country in which there is a high rate of maternal mortality.

Guidance

Look at Table 1.3 on page 8. Citing an African country will persuade the examiner that you are aware of the spatial distribution of this issue.

Using case studies

Naming and using a supporting example

The next level requires that you do more than just name an appropriate example. You will also be expected to demonstrate knowledge and understanding by providing a little detail.

43 Question

Name one country that has been badly hit by the HIV/AIDS pandemic. Give reasons for your choice.

Guidance

Any African country south of the Sahara would be appropriate. Your justification needs to consider a number of criteria for measuring the seriousness of the impact. Quoting some appropriate statistical data — morbidity rate, mortality rate, incidence of orphaned children etc. — will give weight to your choice.

Using case studies comparatively

Essay-type questions that require the comparative use of case studies are popular with chief examiners. In some instances, as below, the comparison is prescribed. In others it is not, and the challenge of such questions is to select appropriate case studies. In some instances, the choice is fairly obvious and restricted. In others, there may be more choice and options than you might think from an initial reading of the question. As a general rule, the more contrasting your case studies, the more you have to bite on.

44 Question

Contrast the UK and the USA in terms of their healthcare systems.

Guidance

The main difference lies in the relative importance of the public and private sectors. Explore differences in the perception of public healthcare provision.

The trouble with all examination questions that ask you to compare situations or places is that most candidates believe that all they have to do is to rehash each in turn. What this really means is that examiners are left to draw their own conclusions as to whether or not the situations are similar. In short, the question is not answered and relatively few marks will be gained. In planning effective answers to the comparative type of question, it is necessary to interleave rather than block references to the situations or places being compared.

Building an essay around a single case study

A successful attempt to answer any question that starts, 'With reference to a named country...' will require you to:

1 choose an appropriate country
2 have a sufficiently detailed knowledge of that country relevant to the thrust of the particular question
3 resist the temptation to set down literally all that you know about your chosen country (the 'kitchen sink' approach), but instead harness only those aspects that are directly relevant

Question
With reference to one country, explain why obesity is described as a health 'time bomb'.

Guidance
Case studies 18 and *43* should help you tackle this question, particularly if you choose the UK. The 'time bomb' analogy requires you to establish the rate at which the incidence of obesity is rising and the risks and costs associated with obesity. As for the latter, the following generic headings should give your answer both structure and coherence.

Physiological and medical
■ Heightened risk of a range of illnesses and early death.
The costs below are essentially the repercussions of the previous bullet point.

Economic
■ Productivity of labour force reduced by days off for ill-health.
■ Labour force deprived of the experience of older workers who die before reaching the age of retirement.
■ Capacity of public transport reduced by having to accommodate larger and therefore fewer people.
■ Coping with obesity — larger clothing sizes, stronger beds and chairs.

Social
■ Overstretched health service.
■ Premature deaths leading to break-up of families and higher incidence of orphans.

Planning an extended essay or report involving a range of case studies

The standard advice on essay planning should be followed, namely that the essay should have a three-part structure — an introduction and a conclusion (say one extended paragraph each) separated by a series of paragraphs (the expansion) that develop your argument or discussion points. It is here that you will need to incorporate supporting examples and case studies. An essential difference between an essay and a report is that the latter should make use of headings, sub-headings and bullet points. The former should be extended prose only, and should not make use of these three report devices.

46 **Question**

Using case studies

To what extent do the causes of health risks vary from country to country?

Guidance

Introduction

Define 'health risk'. Make two brief points, stating that the causes are both physical and human, and noting the basic difference between developing and developed countries in terms of the major health risks — infectious versus non-infectious.

Expansion

Structure your discussion according to a framework of causes, such as:

■ environmental — not just physical, but pollution, housing, hygiene and working conditions
■ national development status
■ population structure — youthful versus ageing
■ lifestyles — poverty versus affluence
■ access to, and quality of, healthcare

Be sure to quote at least one supporting case study for each causal category.

Conclusion

You might attempt an assessment of the relative importance of the causes you have discussed, and perhaps contrast developing and developing countries.

Detecting bias in case studies

We live in an unfair world, and we should always be alive to the fact that what we are reading is not always fair. For example, countries sometimes stand guilty of hiding reality for political reasons — i.e. governments deliberately understate the incidence and impact of a particular disease. For many years, China and South Africa strenuously denied that HIV/AIDS was a problem within their borders.

Writers often write from a personal viewpoint, and as a result what they produce is almost invariably biased towards that viewpoint. Rarely is a particular issue viewed evenly from a range of different viewpoints. Aspects of health in which bias might be expected include the appraisal of healthcare and statistical measures to show that a specific disease is not out of control. It is particularly important when reading case study material to be constantly alive to possible bias — first identify it and then decide what needs to be said to give it balance and a sense of evenness and fairness.

47

With reference to examples, suggest why there might be bias in the reporting of health risks.

Guidance

Why are sources likely to be biased? Think of: the players involved in producing and marketing drugs; governments promoting their welfare policies; healthcare league tables. You might include some research into the deaths at Stafford hospital (2005–08) or the SARS epidemic in the Far East (2003).

Grasping and applying the advice contained in this final part of the book should have a positive outcome. It is sometimes easy to forget that the subject of geography is about the real world. The more contemporary examples you can include in your examination work, the more you are likely to convince and impress the examiner that you have a sound knowledge and understanding of today's world. In short, a good dose of reality in the form of relevant case studies and examples can work wonders when it comes to improving your AS and A2 geography grades.